FORTUITOUS ENCOUNTERS

FORTUITOUS ENCOUNTERS

Wisdom Stories for Learning and Growth

Edited by Paul Davis and
Larry C. Spears

PAULIST PRESS
New York / Mahwah, NJ

Cover and book design by Lynn Else

Library of Congress Cataloging-in-Publication Data.
Fortuitous encounters : wisdom stories for learning and growth / edited by Paul Davis and Larry C. Spears.
p. cm.
SBN 978-0-8091-4805-9 (alk. paper) — ISBN 978-1-58768-084-7 1. Leadership—Case studies. 2. Servant leadership—Case studies. I. Davis, Paul. II. Spears, Larry C., 1955–
HD57.7.F678 2013
650.1—dc23
2012038597

Published by Paulist Press
997 Macarthur Boulevard
Mahwah, New Jersey 07430

www.paulistpress.com

Printed and bound in the
United States of America

CONTENTS

FOREWORD

Storyteller: *Richard J. Leider*

On a business trip to Boston, a cabbie reminds me of how naming your life's calling can make all the difference.

"So, whaddya in town for?" he asks.

"I'm giving a speech. A presentation to some business-people," I say, hoping to make it sound uninteresting so the driver will leave me alone.

He doesn't take the hint. "Oh, yeah? What's it about?"

I'm not interested in giving the speech twice, so I offer the *Reader's Digest* abridged version. "Hearing and heeding your life's calling—doing the work you were born to do."

My cabbie scoffs. "Your life's *calling*? C'mon, I drive a cab here. What's that got to do with a calling?"

I close my folder and catch the driver's eye in the rearview. "You weren't born to drive a taxi?"

He just laughs.

"But you like your work well enough?"

He shrugs. "I guess it has its moments."

"I'm interested. What are those moments?"

"You mean besides quittin' time?"

I lean forward and put my hand on the front seat. "I'm serious. Is there any time you feel like you're bringing all of yourself to what you do?"

He smirks like he's going to say something sarcastic, but then stops. Gradually, his face softens. He laughs a little and says, "Well, there's this old lady."

I stay silent and he continues.

"A couple times a week, I get a call to pick her up and take her to the grocery store. She buys just a couple items. I help her carry them into her apartment, maybe unload them for her in her kitchen. Sometimes she asks me to stay for a cup of coffee. It's no big deal, really. I'm not even sure she knows my name. But I'm her guy. Whenever she calls for a taxi, I'm the guy that goes. And, I dunno, just makes me feel good. I like to help out."

"There's your calling right there," I say.

"What?" The smirk returns. "Unloading groceries?"

"You said you like to help out. That's a pretty clear expression of calling."

A smile spreads across his face. "I guess that's right. Most of the time, I'm just a driver, but when I get that chance to help somebody—as long as they're not some kinda jerk or something—that's when I feel good about this job. So, whaddya know? I got a calling."

He is silent for the rest of the short trip. But I can see his face in the rearview mirror, and even when we hit the midtown traffic, he's still smiling.

That was a few years ago, yet his smile stays with me today and reminds me of an essential truth: the more "purpose moments"—or what's become known as "fortuitous encounters"—that we experience, the more likely we are to find satisfaction and fulfillment in all that we do.

When people seek me out as an executive coach, they often bring questions that will not let them alone, questions that keep them up at night and interrupt their thoughts during the day, questions like, *Can I live a purposeful life? How can I create the life I want to have?* When we begin the coaching process, I always ask them two of my own essential questions as well: *What gets you up in the morning?* and *What keeps you up at night?* Now, I'm going to ask *you* a third question:

What recent fortuitous encounters have had a positive impact on your life?

It's easy to be consumed by our day-to-day busyness. And it's rare to push the pause button long enough to hear another person's story. When we do take the opportunity, our lives are naturally enriched.

Our life is made of days. We cannot shape a whole life. But we can live this *one* day seeking fortuitous encounters.

A friend of mine who has lived in Paris for over thirty years once explained *l'art de vivre* ("the art of living") to me. He said, "Enjoying small things on a daily basis—such as a brisk walk, a favorite café, lovely flowers, sitting in the park, an hour to yourself with a glass of wine, the companionship of a stranger—will help you master the art of living." Great wisdom.

However you decide to use your days, the shape of your days will become the shape of your life. This wise book will serve as a great companion to help you stay awake to the fortuitous people, places, and things that ultimately shape your days and your life.

Richard J. Leider is founder and chairman of The Inventure Group, a coaching and consulting firm in Minneapolis, devoted to bringing out the natural potential in people. He is also the author or coauthor of eight books, including the best sellers Repacking Your Bags *and* The Power of Purpose.

FROM "BIRDS" TO "PEERS"

The Story of Herman Rummelt
and D. J. De Pree

Storytellers:
Paul Davis and Larry C. Spears

A company is rightly judged by its products and
services, but it must also face scrutiny as to its
humanity.

—D. J. De Pree, founder,
Herman Miller Company

Stories have the power to inspire and change lives. The
"Millwright Died," as told by Max De Pree in his book
Leadership Is an Art, is the beautiful true story of how the
death of a man changed the founder of Herman Miller—
Max's father, D. J. De Pree.

D. J. was an entrepreneur who borrowed money from
his father-in-law to buy a small furniture company in West
Michigan. D. J. had the good sense to rename the company
after his father-in-law—Herman Miller. The company rose
from humble beginnings in the 1920s to become a leader in

modern furniture design and one of the most admired companies in America.

D. J. began as a traditional manager of his times. He referred to the employees as "birds," and it was not a term of endearment.

In 1927 a key employee—the millwright Herman Rummelt—died of a sudden heart attack. D. J., as the owner, knew he must pay his respects to the widow. D. J. wrote the following about the fortuitous encounter that changed his life forever:

> You see there were several things about Herman Rummelt that I thought were unusual. One was the handicrafts that he made—primarily for his wife—and that was the first thing that she showed me that morning that he died in 1927. Then the next thing she showed me was this sheaf of poetry in his own handwriting. Then she began to tell me about one of the men who was in his department who had been a machine gunner in World War I and had killed a lot of Germans, and felt he was a murderer and he was going to hell because of that. Well, Herman Rummelt took time to spend with this man; he was the night watchman, and between rounds he would show him from the Bible that there was reconciliation and forgiveness.
>
> So I saw this man [Rummelt] with an interest in the souls of people. He was a craftsman. He wrote poetry. Here were three sides of a person besides his job of keeping that line shaft in good shape.
>
> That was the morning he died. Later after the funeral, as I walked the block and a half from the church to my house, I felt that God was dealing with me about this matter of my attitude toward the

workers in the plant, and I began to realize that we're all alike. Because here was a man that did these things that I couldn't do, or I wasn't doing. By the time I got home, I had decided that we were all extraordinary, and this changed my whole attitude toward what we call "labor"...These people were my peers. [Herman Miller Company Annual Report, 1988, p. 3]

D. J. De Pree was a man of deep faith. He believed that we are all children of God. He believed that part of the lesson of the millwright's death was that we all have talents and that if we spend time together we all have something to learn and something to teach. As children of God, we have talents to share, and any meeting with another human being is important. It just might be a fortuitous encounter.

Others have gone on to describe such meetings as "causeless miracles" or "strange accidents of fortune," but to D. J. De Pree, they were evidence of the hand of God.

The experience of Herman Rummelt's death led D. J. De Pree to develop a set of beliefs and practices that he called "fortuitous encounters." This book of true stories helps to carry forward this important idea into the twenty-first century.

FOR REFLECTION

Do you tend to see most people as ordinary or extraordinary? What would the world be like if we acknowledged the extraordinary in everyone?

UNDERSTANDING FORTUITOUS ENCOUNTERS

Paul Davis and Larry C. Spears

Serendips stroll through dictionaries,
Cookbooks and itineraries.
They trade the cow for the magic bean
And come on treasures unforeseen.
—Betty Bridgman

We have all experienced "fortuitous encounters"—those moments where a person, place, or thing causes our lives to change in a more positive direction.

Our lives are full of what some have called serendipity —strange acts of fortune or causeless miracles. A favorite teacher inspires our choice of career, or a chance encounter develops into love, marriage, and a new family. At the time we are most in need of a friend, one appears. We look at a mountain or the ocean and find meaning and peace. We read a book and an idea is planted in our brains that provides the wisdom we seek.

What if we had never met that teacher? What if we had never met our "significant other"? What if we had not met the friend or mentor who helped us through the rough spots in life? What if we never experienced the beauty of nature? What if we had not read that book? For most of us, the fortuitous encounters of our lives are the parts that contain the most meaning.

In our field of service, leadership, and organizational development, we explore questions like, *What makes some leaders successful while others struggle?* and *What do leaders do to create excellent organizations?* We know that continuous learning is present where there are successful servant-leaders and organizations, and it is absent where leaders and their organizations fail. However, the same could be said for almost all fields that depend on people—the successful continue to learn while those that stop learning fail.

The ability to experience fortuitous encounters is key to learning and growth. The more fortuitous encounters that someone has, the better the odds that the person is successful and happy. While fortuitous encounters are by their very nature a product of chance beyond our ability to control, we strongly believe, as did Pasteur, that "chance favors only the prepared mind." D. J. De Pree believed that the hand of God helped set some fortuitous encounters in motion, but he also followed the advice of Dr. Martin Luther King, Jr., who wrote, "Jesus always recognized that there is a danger of having a high blood pressure of creeds and an anemia of deeds." De Pree believed that a person could increase the odds of experiencing fortuitous encounters by simply being open to their possibilities. Our intention is not to try to explain chance or divine intervention in this book, but simply to help the reader, whatever his or her core beliefs, to understand the power of fortuitous encounters.

In this book, you will read firsthand reports of fortuitous encounters of many kinds. These true stories can help you learn how to prepare yourself to experience your own fortuitous encounters, and experience a lifetime of learning and growth.

FOR REFLECTION

How do you learn? Are fortuitous encounters a part of how we learn? How can you increase fortuitous encounters in your life?

1

DINNER WITH MRS. CORETTA SCOTT KING

Storyteller: *Paul Davis*

Servant-leadership is more than a concept: it is a fact. Any great leader, by which I also mean an ethical leader of any group, will see herself or himself as a servant of that group and will act accordingly.

—M. Scott Peck

My heart pounded as I entered the modest but well-kept-up home of Mrs. Coretta Scott King. I had read all of Dr. King's books. I had read Mrs. King's book. I had watched the movie *From Montgomery to Memphis* about the civil rights movement. I had kept a journal. I had studied nonviolence and read Gandhi's autobiography. I had devoted months to prepare myself, yet nothing really could prepare a white kid from Michigan for my chicken dinner with the first lady of the civil rights movement.

I wanted so much to please her, to thank her for allowing me to be an intern at the Martin Luther King Center. For bearing all the pain and suffering she had experienced with such grace. For making the world a better place.

5

As we sat in her combination kitchen-and-dining room, Mrs. King turned to me while studying the floor and said, "I wish I had carpet." The floor was covered with linoleum.

As the son of a landlord, I knew how to calculate the cost of carpet in my head. I surveyed the room and quickly calculated the number of square feet of carpet she would need. I had just bought carpet not three months before, so I had a good idea of the cost for a wide range of carpets.

"Mrs. King," I said. "I am sure that we could carpet this area for a very reasonable amount and I would be happy to help you."

Mrs. King smiled, and thanked me, but then went on to say, "You don't understand. Martin asked me not to have carpet. The people we wanted to lead are very poor, and carpeting would be considered the height of luxury to them. I don't have carpet because I choose to lead poor people."

During that fortuitous encounter, I learned that leadership is not about what you get by being a leader, but about what you are willing to give up.

FOR REFLECTION

What are you willing to give up in order to lead others? Imagine a world where exemplary leadership is judged on the basis of serving and sacrifice. What fortuitous encounters have you had with this type of leader?

2

BE PREPARED

Storyteller: *Larry C. Spears*

Prepare now for your old age.

—Elmer Davis

I have spent most of my adult life raising awareness about Robert K. Greenleaf and his writings on servant-leadership. Following Greenleaf's death, I gathered his scattered writings and produced and edited the five books for which he is known today.

In *Servant Leadership* (Paulist Press, 1977/2002), Greenleaf wrote, "The servant-leader is servant first." And he offered this as his best test of servant-leadership: "Do those served grow as persons? Do they, while being served, become healthier, wiser, freer, more autonomous, more likely themselves to become servants? And, what is the effect on the least privileged in society? Will they benefit or at least not be further deprived?"

While one of my personal fortuitous encounters was in meeting Robert Greenleaf, one of Greenleaf's fortuitous encounters came when, at the age of forty, he heard radio commentator Elmer Davis say, "Prepare now for your old age." Greenleaf said that he judged Davis to be a true servant and heeded his advice.

Over the course of the next twenty years, from the age of forty to the age of sixty, Robert Greenleaf made several decisions based upon that fortuitous encounter that helped set up the course of his life from the age of sixty to the age of eighty, the years during which he experienced his greatest productivity and most lasting influence. Chief among them were these:

- Greenleaf resolved to stop his frequent business flying and, instead, began to take trains when travel was required. This afforded him the time for reflection that he felt he needed. It also afforded him greater opportunities for conversation with people.
- He began to make his way to people he thought might teach him something, and might "make him stretch."
- He spent two years with Jungian analysts Martha Jaeger and Ira Progoff focusing on the analysis of his dreams. Greenleaf said that these sessions helped to raise his self-awareness and creativity.
- He developed close relationships with several very different institutions: the Menninger (psychiatric) Foundation, the U.S. Air Force, and the National Council of Churches.
- He developed several close friendships with ethics professors, most notably Rabbi Abraham J. Heschel.
- He engaged in an extensive study of the history of the Religious Society of Friends (Quakers), which he said was an important part of his years of preparation, as well as being an enjoyable activity.

In all of this, Greenleaf sought to prepare himself for a future that was not yet clear to him, but the decisions somehow seemed right.

Many years later, he wrote the following:

> In giving some details of my own preparation I am
> not suggesting that what I did would be appropriate
> or possible for anyone else. But of this I am quite
> sure: anyone who thinks of his or her old age as an
> event to be prepared for is more likely to have a
> more fruitful old age than one who has not thought
> that way, regardless of what his or her preparation
> consists of. Whether one's gifts and opportunities
> are great or small, my advice would be, prepare!

He went on to say that serenity may not be what one
achieves in old age; it may be one of the fruits of what one
has learned by preparing while one is young.

Greenleaf wrote this at the age of eighty-two in his last
essay, titled "Old Age: The Ultimate Test of Spirit" (taken
from *The Power of Servant-Leadership*). In it, he said that he
was grateful to many people, including Elmer Davis for his
radio advice some forty-two years earlier.

"Old age is the ultimate test of spirit," wrote Greenleaf.
"Surviving from my Boy Scout experience seventy years ago
is the motto BE PREPARED. I am eternally grateful for it."

FOR REFLECTION

*Like Greenleaf, what might you do to prepare for your old age?
How might this lead to your own fortuitous encounters?*

3
_____

BECAUSE I WANT TO BE!

Storyteller: *Becky Fulgoni*

> You've got a lot of choices. If getting out of bed in
> the morning is a chore and you're not smiling on
> a regular basis, try another choice.
> —Steven D. Woodhull

I am amazed at the amount of power and control people
are willing to give up. I'm not talking about political power,
or about control as in "command and...." I'm talking about
personal power and control in our lives. I'm talking about
the things that *we* get to pick. The choices that *we* get to
make every day. We seem to need and want power and control desperately, and yet we surrender it so easily and completely. You hear it everywhere: *It's out of my hands...It's none
of my business...They won't accept it...That's the way it's always
been....*

   Maybe we turn over control to the world around us
because we don't recognize these junctures as moments of
choice, times that we can consciously take control back
from the world for a moment. We fall into our routines and
forget that we actually are making choices. Each time we are
confronted with a challenge, we choose our response. But
how often are we willing to give it up to "destiny" or "fate"

or "*them*," never accepting the moment to choose for ourselves? It may seem that most of life is out of our control, but we get the chance to take control when we choose our actions and reactions "on purpose."

So, when we wake up and look out on a gray, rainy morning, we can drop our shoulders and mope to the coffeepot for fortification, or we can collect the houseplants and move them out on the porch for the day to enjoy the natural moisture! It's a choice. We pick!

It may sound Pollyannaish (I have been accused of that before) or that I'm "making lemonade," but, as simple as it seems, making purposeful choices is a game changer.

This idea of choosing my reactions to life "on purpose" was driven home for me by my sixteen-year-old son Gus. Every morning Gus gets up (without parental prodding!), showers, collects his things, and finds me (usually trying to pry my eyes open) so he can say, "Have a nice day. I love you," as he heads out the door. It's like clockwork; some might even say relentless! He never seems to "get up on the wrong side of the bed." So one morning my husband asks, "Gus, how come you're always such a happy guy?" Without missing a beat, and with total innocence and candor, Gus replied, "Because I want to be."

Is it really that easy? That simple thought from my teenage son made me realize that I can be ticked-off at the guy who doesn't use his turn signal, or frustrated with the slowpoke in front of me at the bank, or irritated by my coworker who shows up late, but I can also choose *not* to be. That morning I really realized the power in that choice. I also understood in a new way that I have to accept the responsibility to make that choice...on purpose! No one else can choose my happiness, nor can they take it away— it's all on me. I get to pick!

"Because I want to be" has become the mantra in my head that reminds me to choose. To choose to be happy. To choose to be tolerant. To choose to be helpful. To choose to be the change that I want to see in the world (to paraphrase Gandhi). I know that Gus was not trying to be profound; it's just how it works for him. But by seeing each day as an opportunity to choose, he is in control—he has the power! And I'm finding that it's getting easier to see the opportunities that I have to make choices and that it really is that simple.

FOR REFLECTION

Think of times in your life when you were mad or frustrated. Was there an opportunity to choose a different reaction? As a leader, how do you help others choose to be positive? How do you take responsibility for your own choices?

4

THE FARMER

Storyteller: *Paul Davis*

> If I am walking with two other men, each of them
> will serve as my teacher. I will pick out the good
> points of the one and imitate them, and the bad
> points of the other and correct them in myself.
> —Confucius

Steam poured out from under the hood of the old Saab
while I coasted off the highway onto the shoulder.

This didn't look good. It was Sunday morning and it
looked like I would not make the sixty-mile trip from
school to home.

I raised the hood and could see immediately what had
gone wrong. A rubber hose had split, and steam and radiator fluid were pouring out onto the hot engine.

I had no tools, no credit cards, just a well-worn ten-
dollar bill in my pocket. Why did I have to own such an old
car? What was worse, it was old and foreign—with metric
parts and pieces in a land that measured things in inches.

I was in trouble, but fortunately help arrived in the form
of a farmer in a rusted pickup truck. He took one look under
the hood and stated, "You are going to need a new heater
hose. I think I have what you need in my barn." He left and

within fifteen minutes returned with several pieces of hose. However, none of them fit. He said, "I don't have any metric hoses, but I think I can find one that is close enough to work. I need to go back to my farm and look some more."

He left me once again standing beside the old car and drove off. About thirty minutes later, he returned with several more short pieces of hose, this time trimmed to the exact size of my old broken hose. As he predicted, one fit. He had a jug of water that he poured into the radiator. He asked me to start the engine, and he carefully watched to make sure that things were truly fixed and there were no more leaks.

I wanted to thank the farmer who had spent his Sunday morning helping a poor college student get home. I reached into my pocket, found the old ten-dollar bill—all the money I had with me—and I gave it to him.

He looked me in the eye and said, "It's not enough," and my heart fell. I had no more money to give. The farmer said, "Did you like what I did for you?" I said, of course, I liked what he did, and if he gave me his address I would go to the bank on Monday and get him more money. He laughed and said that would be "too easy." He told me to keep my money. What he wanted from me was to stop for others in trouble just as he had done for me.

It has been over forty years since my fortuitous encounter with the farmer. I have stopped countless times for others. Each time the person offers to pay me, I tell them about the farmer and ask the same of them as the farmer asked of me.

FOR REFLECTION

How do you show appreciation for the fortuitous encounters in your life? What are you willing to give to create fortuitous encounters for others?

PASSING THE TORCH

Storyteller: *Larry C. Spears*

> Life is no brief candle to me. It is a sort of splendid
> torch which I have got a hold of for the moment,
> and I want to make it burn as brightly as possible
> before handing it onto future generations.
>   —George Bernard Shaw

On September 20, 1990, I had my one and only fortuitous
encounter with Bob Greenleaf, which occurred just nine days
before his death. I had recently been appointed as the new
director of the Greenleaf Center. Several scheduled trips had
already been planned and postponed during the spring and
into the summer, due to Bob's strokes and related health issues.

At that time, the future of servant-leadership and of the
Greenleaf Center seemed not nearly as strong as they are
today. Awareness of Greenleaf's writings was still mostly
word of mouth, and a few people had voiced doubts to me
as to the likelihood of the Greenleaf Center continuing after
his passing. I was also aware of Bob Greenleaf's own concerns as to his legacy, and so as I planned for what turned
out to be our one and only morning together, I sought to
share with him my vision and insights into what I believed
was a brighter future still to come for the organization that

carried his name. I felt in my bones that servant-leadership was about to blossom all over the world as a result of the many seeds that he had sown in the preceding twenty years, and I shared my ideas with him as to how I thought the Greenleaf Center could be of greater help in nurturing those seeds and many more in the future.

In addition to trying to reassure him about the legacy of his work and his writings, I had also brought dozens of letters that I had received from people who had shared with me just how great an influence servant-leadership and Bob's writings had been to them. With those twin desires in mind to both reassure Bob as to his legacy, and to remind him of the positive difference that he had already made in the world, I drove out from Indianapolis to Kennett Square, Pennsylvania, to Crosslands Retirement Center.

Immediately prior to visiting with Bob, I spent a half hour talking with the social worker who frequently read to him. She told me a bit about his personality traits and his recent life at the center: how his weakening condition and several strokes had caused him great frustration and had seriously limited his ability to speak; how he loved listening to classical music. She mentioned that he was one of the least assuming people she had ever met, and she recounted a story that seemed illustrative of his modest nature: Bob Greenleaf had supposedly once been asked by a new resident at Crosslands what kind of work he had done in the past. Greenleaf, who had retired as director of management research at AT&T, and who went on to become a noted author, lecturer, and consultant to corporations, universities, and foundations, had simply responded, "I worked in an office."

Walking into Bob's room, I found him sitting in his wheelchair and facing the window. He turned his head and smiled and said hello. I sat down in a nearby chair and

introduced myself. As I did, I noticed on his sunny win-
dowsill several pictures, including a picture of my two sons,
James and Matthew, which I had sent to him along with a
birth announcement about Matthew's arrival into the world
two months earlier. Matthew Spears had been born on the
same date as Bob's own birthday—July 14 (Bastille Day!). I
picked up the picture and turned it toward him. He smiled
at me and slowly said, "Nice."

Robert Greenleaf had been concerned in past years
about the continuation of both the servant-leader concept
and the Greenleaf Center. In a letter to the Greenleaf Center
board from the mid-1980s he wrote, "My major concern for
the Greenleaf Center is for its future. I may be hanging up
my sword any day now, and I would like to feel the work I
have done to encourage building greater integrity into our
many institutions will be continued and enlarged in new
directions." It was important to me to share some of the
many positive things that had occurred at the Greenleaf
Center—and to convey my own sense of the ongoing revi-
talization of the Robert K. Greenleaf Center.

Bob had not seen the Center's new office in Indianapolis;
however, we visually walked around it through a series of
black-and-white photographs that I had taken for this purpose. I described the area and building where we were
located at that time, and I showed him the half-dozen liter-
ature cabinets filled with hundreds of copies of his books,
essays, and videotapes. Bob was clearly moved by this visu-
alization of our office, and he stared for a long time at a
photo of a lithograph titled *Terms of Light*, which had been
created by his late wife, noted painter and printmaker Esther
Hargrave Greenleaf.

Greenleaf tenderly examined photocopies of a series of
ten display advertisements that I had recently put together

and that had been placed in various magazines. As Bob heard about the significance of this project—and particularly when he was told that his work and ideas would be reaching a new audience of over a half-million readers through the advertisements in these publications—he chuckled and said, "Good work."

I then read to Bob some heartfelt and laudatory letters that I had received from a dozen different people. As I finished, a look of amazement swept across his face. Bob seemed profoundly touched by hearing these expressions of appreciation from others who had, in turn, been touched by him and his writings. As Quakers, Bob and I found great meaning and comfort in silence, and so we sat quietly together for quite some time.

There was, of course, nothing that he needed to say. It was I who had come to do the saying on behalf of many of us—to remind him of the legacy that he had left each of us—and to thank him for his life's work. I told him of my own appreciation of the opportunity to serve as the Greenleaf Center's own servant-leader. Bob listened as I also told him of the hundreds of people whom I had already met by that time that had been profoundly influenced by the servant-leader concept. I said to him that I believed that his ideas were likely to become increasingly influential in the coming years. He stared intently for a few moments, and then gave a relaxing sigh.

Our single meeting that sunny September day was of great importance to me, personally. Bob's son, Newcomb Greenleaf, suggested that it may also have been of considerable importance to Bob as well, both providing him with a reminder of his positive legacy to the world and of the many lives that he touched for the better during his eighty-six years—as well as communicating the increasing vibrancy of the Center that bears his name, and which he originally founded in 1964 as the Center for Applied Ethics. Newcomb said he thought it possible that following that meeting his father was at last able to let go of any remaining concerns that he may have had, and to assume a greater sense of peacefulness. I like to think that was the case, and I know that for me, our single encounter provided me with a palpable sense of inspiration and purpose that has guided my own work ever since.

I stood up and took Bob's hand in mine, and I thanked him for our time together. He stared thoughtfully at me and slowly said, "Thank you, Larry." As I walked out of his room, I turned around for one final look.

Bob had picked up the Greenleaf Center's newsletter and was slowly turning the page.

FOR REFLECTION

What experiences have you had where you felt like a torch was passed on to you? What experiences have you had where you have passed a torch on to someone else?

6

TRIBAL TALES

Storyteller: *Lane Baldwin*

> If you don't know the trees you may be lost in the
> forest, but if you don't know the stories you may
> be lost in life.
>
> —Siberian Elder

I never expected this to happen: for others to be reading my words about management and business philosophy; or to be training others (who actually want to learn—from me!), teaching what I know about leadership, business, sales, and customer service.

If you had told me even ten years ago (much less twenty or thirty) that I would be sitting at this computer, writing essays on servant-leadership, or working on a book about the subject with one of the world's foremost living authority on it, I would have laughed myself to tears at the thought. *Quit your day job and go do stand-up*, I'd have said, *because you're really funny*. I would never have considered that a series of fortuitous encounters could so thoroughly change my life.

Back then, I identified myself mostly as a professional musician. Music—the writing and performing of it—was my entire life. I was nearing the top of the Mid-Atlantic market and breaking into the national/international arena. I was named a musical ambassador for Washington, DC, and toured parts of Europe in that capacity. Yes, I had a consulting career, but mostly to musicians and bands, helping them build their audience and find more gigs and for better pay. I did branch out into other areas, mostly to help friends who were starting businesses (or trying to save them). Still, in my heart of hearts, I was a musician first and foremost.

But isn't that often the way with truly fortuitous encounters? One moment you're going along in your life, thinking you know exactly where you're going, what you're doing, even who you are. The next moment you turn a corner and run smack into a stranger who turns your life upside down, shakes out all the detritus, clarifies your purpose, and then helps you farther along the path.

Now, you would never think that an overcoat would have much to do with fortuitous encounters or servant-leadership. Yet, whenever I put on a coat, I think of the day I began my journey of discovery about leading others by serving. I think of the day an overcoat changed my life:

In November 1999, I decided I needed a new overcoat. Remembering my father's comments about the quality of service he had received at his local Men's Wearhouse (in Northern Virginia), I found my own local store and went to investigate. The staff was as good as I'd been led to believe, I was impressed by their knowledge and friendliness, and I put a coat on layaway.

Two days later, I returned to swap my layaway for a different style. This time I was assisted by the manager. In truth, I was far more interested in their management philosophy than in which coat I purchased. I wanted to know what they were doing to create such an excellent customer experience. The manager suggested I might want to speak with Owen Freyburg, the district manager for that area, mentioning that Owen would be in the store the following Saturday.

And so, just before lunch on Saturday, I visited Men's Wearhouse for the third time. They say "third time's the charm." In this case, they were right. Owen was a kindly bear of a man, with a quick wit and wonderful sense of humor. I was immediately impressed with his ability to blend his position as a multi-unit manager with his "just one of the guys" demeanor. He was obviously a manager; you could tell by how his eyes took in everything on the sales floor, how he'd step away for a moment to interact with a customer, assist a salesperson in a task, or offer a quiet word to another, pointing out a need. Yet he operated like no manager I'd ever worked for. He was respectful of everyone on the team, quiet in his comments, soft in his corrections, positive and vocal with his praise. In short, Owen was living what I was still striving to achieve. Owen was who I wanted to be when I "grew up" as a businessman and leader.

For more than an hour, Owen was happy to talk about the company's philosophy—its sales and management styles, the kind of people they seek to hire, and how they groom them into service-oriented salespeople and managers. It wasn't long before he used the term *servant-leadership*. I first thought it was an irreconcilable paradox. How can a servant be a leader? I wondered.

Owen explained that the desire to serve others more fully often draws individuals to accept leadership roles. He gave me a brief history of Robert K. Greenleaf and his work, and how serving the interests of the team and its individual members will allow everyone, the manager included, to achieve greater success and personal fulfillment. He showed me how I could create a workplace in which each person could thrive and grow, a workplace that people looked forward to in the morning.

Most surprising was that Owen repeated so many things my father had taught me about serving others. The light above my head blazed like the sun at noon on the Sahara. *This takes everything Dad taught me to a whole new level*, I thought, as Owen went deeper into the philosophy. *If Dad had given me an education in serving others, working at Men's Wearhouse would be graduate school. Squared.*

At the end of our conversation, Owen said that if I had any questions I was welcome to contact him. "I do have one question," I said. "When can I start?"

Owen laughed and asked, "Start what?"

"I want to work here," I explained. "This is exactly the kind of company I want to be a part of."

I told Owen that, while I didn't know it, I'd been following much of the servant-leader philosophy for years, thanks to my father's guidance. I explained that I had followed the principles of true service-based sales since childhood and wanted to learn how it applied to a large corporation and to managing others. After a lot of back and forth, Owen finally asked me why I thought I'd be a good clothing salesman.

"As you noted earlier," I said, "it's not so much about the product as it is about the salesperson's attitude toward his customers. I've got that attitude ingrained in me, but I know you can teach me even more. I want that education; I want to serve others better. Plus, I'm not afraid to ask for the sale again, just like I'm going to ask you again right now: When can I start?"

I began my work at Men's Wearhouse the following Wednesday, training for three days at the Richmond area location, then standing my first day on their sales floor that

Saturday. From the very beginning, I knew I'd made the right choice.

The early training merely underlined things I already knew, but we quickly moved into new territory, especially regarding the management of others. I already had experience as a manager, and had followed the core servant-leader principles without knowing it. But this was so much more— an entire management philosophy built on the concept of first serving the interests of others and helping them to succeed. I was in management heaven!

During my short tenure as a salesman (MW calls them "wardrobe consultants"), I worked hard to be a strong team member. At the same time, I worked very hard to be the store's best salesperson and one of the best in my district. I took my turn at cleaning bathrooms, sweeping the tailor's shop, making coffee, all the grunt work required to run a good store. I read everything I could find about the company's management style and their sales program, and had numerous conversations with Owen and others. Within weeks, I had learned the program so thoroughly that I could not only quote it chapter and verse, I began to train others on the team.

I admit I was difficult to ignore. I was vocal in my devotion to the sales program in the face of others' resistance to it. Then I outsold them all. Every week for thirteen weeks, I exceeded at every measurement the company tracked, regularly standing in the top five regionally in all categories, occasionally making it into the top twenty nationwide. I also received more registered customer compliments than Owen and the regional manager had ever received for any salesperson, much less a rookie.

Over those first few months, I learned that while the store was in many ways far superior to the company's competition, it was at the bottom of the region's list in terms of actualizing the company's philosophy and sales strategy. Sales were well below expectations, trending lower than the past two years. Customer service was sometimes less than stellar. There were leadership issues, and team members were often at odds with each other. Owen served the district, but, in short, the team itself needed a true servant-leader or it would continue to underperform. I decided the only way to help change the status quo was to accelerate my plan to become a servant-leader—to give the team what it so desperately needed.

Two months after I started (shortly after Christmas), the current store manager confided that he was going to leave the company at the end of January for a higher-paying job. Let me stress that the manager was an excellent salesman and a very nice person. I liked him a lot. But I do know he's much happier having taken that other job, which allowed him to be what he loved most—a salesman, and a very good one.

The day the outgoing manager gave his notice, I was prepared. As he and Owen came back from the meeting at which he announced his departure, I walked Owen right back out the door to ask for the manager's position. I didn't know it at the time, but what I was asking for had only been done once before. MW managers are expected to train for some time, and then serve as assistant manager—often for several years—before being given the keys to a store of their own, along with the responsibility of a multi-million-dollar business.

During that initial interview, I offered several pages of notes detailing the issues facing the store and offering solutions based on servant-leadership and the company's own training. Owen was astounded by my thoroughness as well as my adherence to strict company policy. In fact, even though he told me not to expect success, he agreed to take my case to the regional manager. The only reason he considered it at all was that there was no one else in the area to consider. It was well known that the current assistant manager would not be with the company much longer, and the assistant at the other area store was rather new. So, with no option but a dark horse with no track record—albeit a pretty well-prepared dark horse—Owen did what no sane man should ever do. He bet the farm on long odds.

By the time I interviewed with the regional manager, with Owen there for support, my notes had become a veritable book, filled with assessments, strategies, implementations, tracking, and corrective options. Both men were amazed, and the regional manager asked if he could keep the notes. He said he wanted to use them as a template, using much of what I had written to improve his other stores. He didn't agree to my request, however. Instead, he "kicked it upstairs" to the top executives, including founder and CEO George Zimmer and the EVP of operations, Charlie Dressler. Much to Owen's surprise, the two agreed to make me a temporary manager with a ninety-day probationary period. Owen later said it was the book that tipped it. I've heard that it was actually Owen that did, doubling down on his bet by putting his own reputation—and career—on the line for me.

Let me pause here for a moment and consider the many ways that Owen demonstrated true servant-leadership, time and again living the ideal in his service to me. First, he educated me. Then, he took a chance on me and gave me a job. Then he took the time to mentor me, teaching me every facet of the service process as well as the management theory and application that drove the company. He told the "tribal tales" as Max De Pree calls them, instructing me in the history that made the company great, what made it a servant-led company.

Consider that when Owen recommended me to the regional manager—his boss—he was gambling his own credibility as a multi-store manager. He had to take full responsibility for his choice, accepting all the potential negative consequences if I failed. Compound that by the fact that, in persuading his boss to recommend me, he was asking his boss to do the same, and put his name on the decision. Owen not only bet the farm, he got his more highly placed neighbor to do the same. Then, in that final meeting, which took place in California during the district's annual managers' meeting, Owen reiterated his commitment to CEO George Zimmer himself.

Without Owen's guidance and then faith, I may well not have continued my career with the company when, about a year later, I had to relocate to another state. Thankfully, however, he led me by serving my best interests, by allowing me to grow to my greatest potential. And most of all, he stood by me when I needed that support in order to gain the next step in the journey.

Throughout my stint as manager of the Midlothian store, Owen was always there when I needed him. His guidance was instrumental to my success and, more important, to my growth as a servant-leader. I am very proud that, in one short year, that store team went from being one of the lowest performers in the district to "Top Store Team." That team registered more compliments in a six-month period than any other store had ever achieved. Only a real team— one that is focused on mutual success—can achieve something like that.

Michael Bass, one of the young salespeople I mentored, became my assistant manager and now manages that same store. I championed Michael for promotion to assistant only three months after my own rise to manager. What convinced Owen to approve my request was when I told him that I wanted to pay his gamble on me forward to Michael.

"I know he can do it, Owen," I said firmly. "He'll do it and he'll make us both very proud, or I'll take the hit. My call. My responsibility."

Owen smiled and said yes. And we are both very proud. The store continues to perform very well, and is definitely led by a true servant-leader. I still call Michael from time to time, because it's important to remember the beginning, and our fortuitous encounters. Don't you agree?

FOR REFLECTION

How has a fortuitous encounter encouraged you to take the personal risks necessary to improve the company you work for?

7

TRUE SERVICE

Storyteller: *Lane Baldwin*

I slept and dreamt that life was joy. I awoke and
saw that life was service. I acted and behold, service was joy.

—Rabindranath Tagore

When my spouse was relocated to New Jersey, I went with
her. I'd been a Men's Wearhouse store manager in Virginia.
In my new region, I was assigned to a store that was having
some difficulties. I worked with management there to
rebuild the team for several months before then becoming
co-manager of a newly opened store. My co-manager Irving
Wright went on to manage the Wall Street store when it
opened. Although we spent less than a year together, Irv was
instrumental in easing my transition into an entirely different type of market. The mindset was completely different:
not just the customers, the salespeople were different as
well. This meant I had more to learn, and Irv, with a career
built in the area, was the perfect teacher.

I'll note that Larry Berkowitz and Ralph Russo (my district and regional managers) were also both excellent mentors. But it was that daily work with Irv that provided the
foundation. Together we mentored several up-and-coming

managers. One took over a highly prestigious and sought-after store. Others took larger stores as well. Later, I continued to mentor within the company and still keep tabs on many of those friends.

Even after I left the Virginia region, my original Men's Wearhouse mentor Owen Freyburg continued to stand by me. His support and guidance helped me settle into my new home and continue to succeed—and learn. With Owen's encouragement, I submitted an article on service to the internal newsletter. The article was the beginning of a column I wrote for two years, telling others what I knew about offering top-flight customer service to our patrons. It was also the fortuitous encounter that led to the change in my role at Men's Wearhouse.

I realized that moving every few years (following my then wife's career path) would prevent me from advancing beyond store manager. Having been bitten by the writer's bug, I applied to become a part of the team creating the company's new interactive Web site. My thought was to attempt to create a position I could fill from home as a telecommuter. I had even heard that there were others already doing it.

Kirk Warren, VP of benefits, was heading the project at the time. At first, he resisted my request. Kirk said he had not had much success working with telecommuters. (His office is in Fremont, California, on the opposite side of the country.) Other telecommuters were not producing results and were hard to track. Initially, he agreed to let me write for him part-time, during my off hours. He gave me a few assignments that I returned within forty-eight hours. He gave me four more and I finished them over the weekend.

After that, Kirk agreed to take me on full-time, but with reservations. During the phone call in which he made the offer, he repeatedly expressed his misgivings about the entire concept. In fact, he was so outspoken that I hung up wondering if I should take the job at all! Kirk told me to sleep on it. The next day, I called him back and expressed my own concern. Only then did I realize that he had, in a sense, set me up.

Kirk clearly demonstrated his own servant-leadership, beginning with that very real expression of his own concerns. He was honest with me about the issues we both faced, should I accept the position. He wanted me to be aware of the hurdles he'd discovered. Telecommuting was still a relatively new concept, and Men's Wearhouse's first experience with it wasn't doing so well. Certainly the employees themselves shared much of the responsibility for that, but Kirk was willing to admit that he owned at least some of it. By shocking me as he had, he'd given us both the best chance that I'd really look at the entire affair in the proper light, one that illuminated the challenges so we could address them—together.

After making that point at the beginning of the second call, Kirk set the stage for us to begin our exploration of the issues, and the solutions. He did this by actively listening to my worries, then addressing them one at a time. By the end of that second call, we had devised a plan that would allow us to resolve each issue and provide the ongoing contact Kirk wanted. As we progressed, we refined our original plan—again, as a cooperative exercise. In addition, Kirk provided me with much-needed guidance on this new, unusual style of writing. We had daily discussions morning and evening, and we learned together how to build a strong telecommuting relationship. In fact, we virtually wrote our own "operations manual" on the subject, one that I follow to this day, albeit with revisions and refinements.

This education in long-distance relationships is an extra bonus on top of the servant-leadership advantages. Ever since I left the company, I have worked both careers—as a businessman and a musician—using the things I learned with Kirk. Today I serve David Nordschow Amplification as vice president of sales and related areas, and do it from my home office, where I sit typing this essay. I also manage my music career, my band's operations, booking, and recording, two young charities with delusions of national growth, a continuing consulting practice, and my speaking and writing on servant-leadership—all from a small room in my home, using e-mail, phone, and text to stay in touch with thousands of people. Had it not been for my work with Kirk, none of this would be possible.

FOR REFLECTION

How has a fortuitous encounter given you a chance to do something you would not have been able to do before the encounter?

8

SUITING UP FOR THE BIG GAME

Storyteller: *Lane Baldwin*

Tell the child, Look, I love you, I believe in you. I
know you are going through a lot of upset.... The
only thing that counts is that in the long run, you
find out who you are and you live it.

—Rollo May

In the beginning, I worked for several months on sales copy
for the Men's Wearhouse Web site—short paragraphs to
help sell their clothing. Later, I worked with Tom Ogle, customer service director, on the "customer assistance" portion
of the site—the help pages, FAQ files, and informational
pages that answer customer questions. Tom taught me a lot
about customer service and problem solving. I owe much of
my current sales/service philosophy to the time he took to
polish my rough edges. He is a master at saying "I'm sorry,"
then making it right. Let's face it: Even in the finest organizations, things are going to go wrong from time to time.
Tom helped me understand my challenging customers better, and gave me the tools to rectify almost any wrong. He
taught me that the complaining customer on the other end
of the phone took the time to call because they want to find

a way to continue doing business with you. All you have to do is help them succeed at that.

"Be grateful for the ones who call, Lane," he said one day. "It's the ones who don't call that you should worry about, because you never get a chance to repair the relationship. The callers *want* to repair it."

Tom's guidance taught me how to more fully incorporate servant-leadership concepts into my relationships with customers and clients. When it comes down to it, true service-based sales—which I now call True Service—is based on the same values, philosophies, and goals as servant-leadership. I had already discovered that on my own, but Tom helped me greatly expand my thinking in this regard.

At the same time, Kirk Warren, who had originally headed up the project of creating the new Web site, continued to teach me servant-leadership in the best way: he lived it daily. His patient, caring management turned me into a credible corporate copywriter. The hours we spent discussing servant-leadership and humanistic management reinforced my father's lessons and significantly built on them. When we completed the sales work on the store portion of the site, Kirk invited me to work with him on benefits, operations, and training manuals. This work gave me keen insight into the proper care of employees. I learned that it's quite different—and a much greater challenge—to oversee a large company with thousands of employees. Looking back now, I'm amazed at the sheer amount of information he offered me.

I had met George Zimmer, founder of the Men's Wearhouse, earlier at the holiday parties the company held annually in every region. He knew who I was, first because of my initial request to become a store manager less than three months after I had first been hired as a floor salesman, and then later because of my work in various regions.

(George once joked he'd written so many congratulatory memos to me and my teammates that he was going to buy a rubber stamp to sign his name!) However, I had never worked directly for him. George and Kirk were beginning to write articles for a business philosophy section of the site, and invited me to write with them. You could call this my postdoctoral work in servant-leadership, and one of my most important fortuitous encounters. Now, servant-leadership philosophy had become the very core of my work. All I did for eight to ten hours a day was read, listen, learn, and write servant-leadership. It was fantastic!

To be honest, it was also a bit daunting to know that I'd be working for, and writing with, the founder of a billion-dollar company. I soon saw firsthand that George was truly the source of servant-leadership at Men's Wearhouse. All those things I'd heard about him—how he put his employees first, how he'd lavishly rewarded those who helped the company survive economic upheaval in Texas in the early days, how he would chip in to help with the dirtiest, most menial tasks—were true. In our first meeting, *he* poured *my* coffee!

George spent the first fifteen minutes of that meeting asking about my life. Not my work, but my personal life: "How long have you been married? How do you like the Northeast? What kind of music do you enjoy? What do you do for fun?" I don't know about you, but this wasn't how I expected my "short" meeting with the Boss to go. I expected five to ten minutes of receiving instructions and back out the door. Instead, we were pushing twenty minutes, George was offering more coffee, and all we'd done was talk about me.

George was a wonderful leader; he knew to take the time to get to know me, and to make me feel at ease in his inner sanctum before getting down to business. When we did move into work mode, George quickly demonstrated not only his vast knowledge of servant-leadership, but also his sincere commitment to follow the principles at all times. I came away from that meeting with the realization that I was going to learn from a master of servant-leadership implementation.

As time went on, I didn't see George that much, but he sure knew what I was doing. He read every word I wrote and had very helpful comments to offer. He also offered a large measure of encouragement. Kirk continued to be my main contact and my direct supervisor. However, our roles changed slowly during this period. Kirk was confident enough in himself to allow me to grow as a writer and editor. We became coeditors, each of us editing the other, with many hours devoted to discussing the philosophies about what we wrote. He never stopped encouraging me to stretch my capabilities, and was always there to lend a hand if I got in a bit too deep.

My work with Kirk offered numerous other fortuitous encounters with some of the world's most important thinkers in management, team building, and positive living, including Rinaldo Brutuco, Joseph Simonetta, Mark Albion, and many others. Each of these people had an impact on me, adding to my education in servant-leadership specifically, and what some call right livelihood in general. Every time I turned around, I was introduced to someone else and their work.

Think kid in a candy store.

FOR REFLECTION

How has a fortuitous encounter led to a longterm mentor in your life? How has a fortuitous encounter led you to mentor others?

9

THANKFULNESS

Storyteller: *Lane Baldwin*

At times our own light goes out and is rekindled
by a spark from another person. Each of us has
cause to think with deep gratitude of those who
have lighted the flame within us.
—Albert Schweitzer

Larry Spears had led the Robert K. Greenleaf Center for
ServantLeadership for a decade or so by the time I first
spoke with him. Obviously, being neck-deep in servant-
leader philosophy, Larry would be an important person
from whom to learn. He kindly took the time to further
educate me and to introduce me to many new resources.
One thing that impressed me immediately was his willing-
ness to work with me—someone whom he did not know.
He took me under his wing for a time and taught me to fly.

After I left Men's Wearhouse, Larry and I maintained occasional contact. Every so often, I'd write or call. I had decided to
expand my consulting practice again, and wanted to integrate
all I had learned into my work. Larry offered some very timely
advice, and also encouraged me to continue writing.

The next several years of my life were tumultuous, to
say the least: I survived a dreadful divorce and a subsequent

bout of major depression; moved across the country to seek healing; moved a second time in less than a year, this time more than a thousand miles to the middle of corn country; faced a serious upheaval in my musical career; and suffered through a second divorce. I continued to maintain contact with Larry, but it was sporadic, occurring in the few "good times" over those years. Whenever I contacted him, however, whether by phone or e-mail, Larry always had time to talk with me, advise me, and encourage me to keep going. His positive voice and spirit were a bigger help than he realizes.

By the time 2009 rolled around, we had renewed regular contact. I refocused on my writing and speaking, and accepted ordainment as an interfaith spiritual minister. Having survived the most difficult period of my life, I determined to take everything I had learned about serving others and to use it in every way I could.

No one was more excited for me than Larry. We began to talk more, and Larry continued to encourage me and offer guidance. We finally met face to face in April 2009 at Larry's home. It was a wonderful day, and one I'll never forget. Larry invited me to write with him—not *for* him, *with* him. We talked about several concepts and agreed to pursue the idea. In 2010, Larry invited me to join the board of the Spears Center for Servant-Leadership.

I still consider myself a musician as much as a servant-leader. The beautiful thing, however, is that I get to do them *together*. I am a servant-leader to all the musicians with whom I have worked over the years. As an artist-relations representative for several companies, I deal with hundreds of professional artists each year. I also interact with thousands of semi-pros, hobbyists, and students at all levels. As the main sales representative for David Nordschow Amplification, I interact with hundreds of dealers and corporate sponsors. And more than anything, I seek to serve them all to the best of my ability.

Recently, I have begun using my music in presentations on servant-leadership (where appropriate), and incorporating the servant-leadership model into every facet of my work, even as I promote it to anyone who'll listen. During concerts, my servant-led band, Deeper Blues, shows the audience how to use the blues to find renewal and strength while entertaining them. We perform at various charity events. I also founded a charity based on a benefit we did to celebrate the release of our first CD. Danville Foodstock was a direct result of my desire to set an example of servant-leadership in my community. In three years (before I moved again), we sponsored several benefit concerts and food drives in support of the Danville Area Food Pantry, offered a free monthly dinner to all, and delivered dozens of meals each month to those who could not attend.

In May 2010, I cofounded Low Notes for Nashville, offering relief to musicians devastated by the worst flood in Nashville history. Led by my close friend Sean O'Bryan Smith, Low Notes has attracted an international following and has donated more than $50,000 to help fellow musicians recover their lives. This work allows me to serve a larger community and to practice the important trait of servant-followership, which is crucial to the success of the servant-leader.

Even in my ministry (small though it is), I promote servant-leadership, often using Jesus, Buddha, Gandhi, and many others, as examples of how similar servant-leadership philosophy is to so many spiritual paths. Everywhere I turn, I find a new way to use servant-leadership to help create a "more just, more caring society," as Greenleaf put it so long ago. Every day offers another opportunity to serve, and every service brings with it a sense of fulfillment unlike any other I know.

"The road goes ever on and on," recites Bilbo Baggins in J. R. R. Tolkien's *The Lord of the Rings*, as he leaves his home for Rivendell. His nephew Frodo later recounts a comment Bilbo made years before: "You step onto the Road, and if you don't keep your feet, there is no knowing where you might be swept off to." In both cases, Bilbo is right. Sometimes you just don't know where the road will take you. But if you're lucky, you'll have a fortuitous encounter—or a "Wearhouse" full of them!—to help you along the way.

Often, the most important encounters can begin quite innocently. It's seldom that the clouds simply part and the sun shines down upon you to announce such an encounter. Billboards don't flash, and bands don't strike up a march. And that is the final thought I would like to offer—that you never know when the fortuitous encounter will occur, or with whom it might be. Sometimes it's the little things that lead to great change. The greatest symphony begins with a single note. A short phrase echoes throughout the hall, suggesting the beauty to come. More notes, and a hint of rhythm. A pause as the orchestra takes in a collective breath, and suddenly…Mozart!

The only way to notice these quiet, unobtrusive offers is to listen with your heart and spirit, to be open to the very possibility that it can happen for you—and it will, if you let it.

I am supremely grateful for every encounter with the people I've mentioned in my essays here. Each of them has changed my life for the better. I have a greater purpose and sense of mission than ever before. A clearer vision and a stronger belief in myself. A stronger desire to serve others, and a far greater sense of fulfillment in so doing. I live a vibrant life, filled with beauty and love, doing what I love most—playing music and helping others. I am truly a lucky man, and I owe so much to those who have helped me along the way. Yes, I am exceedingly grateful.

Even more so, I am grateful that I once needed a new overcoat!

FOR REFLECTION

How do you show appreciation and thankfulness in your life? How can a grateful spirit lead to more fortuitous encounters? How do small encounters built over time become a fortuitous life?

10

THE MOTTO

Storyteller: *Myron Marsh*

And gladly would he learn and gladly teach.
                                    —Geoffrey Chaucer

I began 1970 in a place that I never imagined, a university.
Throughout my high school education I had been counseled
that my aptitude and interest were best suited to a career in
industry. So I diligently pursued that direction, finally ending
up with the perfect opportunity at Caterpillar Tractor
Company in Peoria, Illinois. The only problem—nothing in
school prepared me for unchallenging work, loss of my identity in a five-thousand-employee plant, labor unrest, a tyrant
supervisor, and the night shift. I lasted six months.

Now what? I was lost...I didn't know what I could,
should, or wanted to do next. The first person I sought for
help was a teacher that I had admired for the past four years.
In my senior year, I had assisted him with a couple of the
entry-level metal-shop classes, and I guess he thought I had a
natural ability to teach others. He painted a vision of what
was possible and provided real encouragement. That was
enough to propel me into a late start at his alma mater,
Illinois State University.

During the four years that I was at Illinois State, I cannot count the number of times that I saw the university motto on signs and letterhead. "And gladly would he learn and gladly teach" was everywhere on everything. It's amazing how oblivious you can be to something right in front of you. The words were there, but I never considered their meaning. Fortunately, knowing the university motto was not a prerequisite for obtaining a degree. After four years, I had gained enough knowledge (or maybe it was just age) to begin my teaching career as a high school shop instructor. This was the profession that I practiced for the next three years. It wasn't the students or the teaching that caused me to make my next career change. I just didn't enjoy the school politics.

I remembered the training programs at Caterpillar Tractor Company and the instructors who taught those classes. So I combined that learning and the teaching skills from Illinois State and embarked on a career in industry. Maybe my career counselors were correct…I was cut out for industry. I just needed to take a different route to get there. I was young and the future was bright. I was fortunate and had many good mentors, and some great bosses along the way. I progressed from being a training coordinator, to playing various human-resource roles, and ultimately became an operations manager. I did not know it, but there was a theme beginning to arise in each of these career moves. To those I worked for and around, I was becoming known as a participative manager. Maybe I was still rebelling against my first tyrant supervisor, but I made an extra effort to engage others in decisions that affected them. I'm not sure I understood why I adopted the style of management that I chose, but my early teaching experience certainly influenced it in some way.

Sometimes you just need to sit back and reflect on your real passions and real reasons why you do some of the things you do. I remember the trigger point that helped my understanding was an opinion editorial that I read in a trade magazine. The author explained that his day consisted of learning and teaching and not managing. Ah ha! That's my driver…learning and teaching. All of a sudden, that motto that I saw so often in the early 70s came alive and had meaning. That's what I do. Those are my passions: I love to learn, and I love to help others learn.

The motto became my mission statement and helped me put my work into focus with perspective. Every day was an incredible learning experience for me, and instead of managing or leading, I was teaching. Things I took for granted took on new meaning. It was no longer about managing a factory. The people I worked alongside became more of a priority: "If they grow, the business will take care of itself." The metrics for employees became one of change, what they were learning—how they were preparing for the future and not how much they were doing.

Don't get me wrong. We didn't ignore profits, customer service, quality, and so on. Those are actually metrics for how much we are learning. And it is that new knowledge or skill that gives us the ability to improve our organizations. It is a different way to look at familiar things. So much I had touched in the past took on a whole new level of understanding and with this, a new opportunity. I had read Peter Senge's book *The Fifth Discipline*; now the premise of creating a "learning organization" started to take on new meaning.

I spent many years trying to make business a rational environment for the people. Now, I felt a validation for my approach and was excited to feel more focused. Besides an enormous amount of learning, I was teaching. Everything changed; meeting agendas were really lesson plans, meetings were teaching opportunities, and telling was replaced with asking. Socrates was a master teacher, and I have always admired teachers that have mastered his method of teaching. Socrates said, "I know you won't believe me, but the highest form of Human Excellence is to question oneself and others." The ability to ask the right questions in turn helps people grow through their own answers. Employees become more engaged through questions than direction.

It took fifteen years until I realized my university motto had really been a fortuitous encounter. With that understanding, my work became rewarding and much more productive. As time passes, it's not the "things" we remember or cherish the most; it's the people, and their successes that are most satisfying. I gladly learn and teach.

FOR REFLECTION

What is your personal mission, motto, or brand? How do you live this mission? What gift have you given to people that you have encountered along life's journey? What knowledge or skill do you "passionately" want to share with others?

11

NIGHT AT THE DANCE

Storyteller: *Paul Davis*

He who teaches a boy teaches three: a youth, a
young man, and an old man.

—German Proverb

My wife and I had just arrived at the neighborhood dance,
held in the local school, when the DJ announced that he
was taking a fifteen-minute break and that refreshments
were being served in the lobby.

As we entered the lobby, we heard a horrible sound. A
neighbor collapsed and his head hit the ceramic tile floor
with a thud I will never forget.

In an instant, the party was over. We looked at each
other. We looked at the man on the floor, hoping that he
would soon get up. We waited for a doctor to appear from
within the crowd of onlookers to tell us what to do.

While we waited in panic, the man at our feet began to
turn blue.

Call 911, someone shouted.

He isn't breathing, someone else shouted.

Can't somebody do something? someone sobbed.

I knelt down beside the man. He wasn't breathing. I
couldn't find a pulse.

Does anyone know CPR? I shouted.

A man appeared.

I'll do the breathing; you do chest compressions, I said. As we started to work, people started shouting advice—all of it wrong.

I said, You do five compressions, then I will breathe, and we will keep that rhythm until he recovers or we are relieved.

My partner found the right spot on the man's chest and began a steady up-down compression.

One, two, three, four, five, he yelled.

I checked to see if anything was in the blue man's mouth, then tilted his head back, pinched his nose, and blew into his mouth.

As the air rushed from me into him, I could taste the spaghetti that he'd had for dinner.

On and on we went:

One, two, three, four, five—breathe.

One, two, three, four, five—breathe.

Where was help? What was taking so long?

A shout from the crowd: The ambulance went to the wrong school. But they are on their way now. Don't stop.

One, two, three, four, five—breathe.

How long can this go on? I thought. I am scared. What if he dies? Is he beginning to turn pink? Yes, he is beginning to turn pink.

My legs were cramping, my back was aching, but we couldn't stop. My whole world was one, two, three, four, five—breathe. I had no concept of time or space, no real sense of what I was doing. My brain had stopped working; everything was one, two three, four, five—breathe.

Finally the crowd parted and two medics arrived with a stretcher. We couldn't be bothered. In our world, it was still one, two, three, four, five—breathe. The medic put his hand on my shoulder and told me that my work was done. They were there to take over.

The next thing I remember was sitting in a hallway crying. Who was the blue man? Would he make it? I just wanted to get home as fast I could. I was physically and mentally spent.

About a month after the night at the dance, the phone rang. On the other end was the blue man's wife.

Thank God, she said. I found you. I did not know who you were, and it has taken me this long to track you down. Thank you for saving my husband. Because you started CPR so soon, he had no heart damage from his heart attack. He is making a full recovery. Would you be willing to come to dinner in your honor at our house?

A few days later, my wife and I, and my partner in CPR and his wife, found ourselves dining with the blue man and his family. His beautiful daughters served us a wonderful meal. We were the heroes of the hour. We were special. We were appreciated.

But I began to feel guilty. I could hardly remember the night at the dance. I had been so scared I could barely move, and time had not made that night any clearer to me. I began to realize where *one, two, three, four, five—breathe* had come from. It had come from a scoutmaster in my hometown. It had come from a fortuitous encounter I had had with a man who had spent his evenings with a gangly bunch of teenagers, teaching them CPR on a dummy he had borrowed from the hospital where he worked. The blue man, his wife, and his daughters were thanking the wrong person, I realized.

I went home, called information, and found the phone number of the scoutmaster whom I had not talked to in over thirty years. He had long since retired from his job at the hospital. I thanked him for the fortuitous encounter he had set in motion. I told him about the blue man and his family. I thanked him for teaching his skills in CPR and told him that his efforts had made a difference.

He said, Thank you for calling, but he did not seem surprised. He somehow knew that the lessons he taught would be used.

FOR REFLECTION

What do you have to teach? How do you know when a lesson has been taught? How does being a teacher create fortuitous encounters for others?

12

AWAKENING DREAM

Storyteller: *Larry C. Spears*

> Your vision will become clear only when you look
> into your heart. Who looks outside, dreams. Who
> looks inside, awakens.
>
> —Carl Gustav Jung

Bill Bottum was the kindest of men, an exemplary servant-leader, and a dear friend.

Starting in 1990 and up until Bill's death in 2005, I visited with him several times a year. Usually I would drive up to Ann Arbor and spend a weekend at his home, with Bill and his beloved Olivia, who died in 1998. My visits with Bill meant much to me, and I have so many wonderful memories: of our many conversations and dinners together at various Ann Arbor restaurants; of celebrating with a bottle of Asti Spumante in 1995 upon receiving word while at his home that the Greenleaf Center had received a big grant from the W. K. Kellogg Foundation; and of long, philosophical conversations in his living room or down in his library. I had also so enjoyed being able to include an essay of his within *Insights on Leadership* in 1998, which he cowrote with Dorothy Lenz. Of our last meeting in late December 2004, I recall Bill's twinkling eyes as he listened to our mutual friend, George SanFacon, and me discuss ideas and books together. Bill's body was giving out on him, but there was a joyful spirit in his eyes.

Bill Bottum also served as an exemplary board trustee for the Robert K. Greenleaf Center for Servant-Leadership for twenty years, from 1981 to 2001. When declining health forced him to withdraw from the board, I felt his absence as a huge hole.

As my friendship with Bill deepened over the years, something similar was taking place between George SanFacon and Bill. The three of us shared a keen commitment to servant-leadership, and each of us had our own special interests in it. Among other things, servant-leadership resonated with Bill's longtime interest in the Beatitudes and their applications for business. George had a deep and abiding commitment to the "Council of Equals" model that Robert Greenleaf described in *The Institution as Servant*, and for many years, George led the Housing Facilities Department at the University of Michigan, using that approach. My own interests in servant-leadership were focused on their meaning for individuals, as well as their being the mission of the Greenleaf Center, which I led as president and CEO from 1990 to 2007.

Over the years, Bill spoke frequently of the work that George was doing, and he would occasionally invite me to look for ways that George and I might collaborate. Bill told me that he thought that George and I could make a good team. Later, I learned from George that Bill had also been telling George of my own work, and that he had also encouraged George to look for ways that the two of us might support one another in our efforts. Due to Bill's sowing of seeds, that eventually happened.

While George SanFacon and I had known each other since the early 1990s, it wasn't until after Bill's death that our relationship began to grow from colleagues to friends. George and I began to spend more time together, and out of that friendship have come a number of collaborative projects.

I had never put much stock in dreams or in analyzing their meaning. Still, in 2006 I had essentially the same dream within a matter of a few days. In this dream, I felt a great urgency to visit Bill's home in order to look for something; next, I was in Bill's home and found myself looking around for undiscovered writings by Bill. In both instances, I awoke from these dreams with the uneasy feeling that I needed to do something. This feeling persisted for several months, until I was finally prompted to act upon it.

Now, my rational mind told me that there were several good reasons why I had had the dreams, and that there was no reason to make too much of them. For one thing, some fifteen years earlier I had had the most unusual experience of discovering nearly one hundred previously unknown writings by Robert Greenleaf, when I went through his personal papers following his death. Greenleaf had found writing down his thoughts to be a useful way for him to understand better his own thinking on many different topics. Over a period of almost fifty years, he would occasionally put down on paper his thinking about something, and then he would simply file it away. Following Greenleaf's death in 1990, I went through his personal papers and found dozens and dozens of files containing documents and manuscripts that ranged from mere one or two pages to one that was over one hundred pages long. The existence of many of these writings had not been known to either his family or friends. Eventually, several of us edited many of these papers, and they were published in two books of new writings by Robert Greenleaf in 1996 (*On Becoming a Servant-Leader* and *Seeker and Servant*). Having had this unusual experience of discovering Greenleaf's private writings some years earlier probably had a good deal to do with these dreams about Bill Bottum.

It is also likely that the dreams were triggered, in part, because of my having read three lengthy documents that Bill had written over the years. In particular, he had written and revised a monograph on the Beatitudes over a period of several decades. The monograph, titled *Within Your Reach*, was something that he had had privately printed and then had given away to thousands of people. In many ways, he viewed that monograph as being at the heart of his important work on this earth. Because I was well aware of *Within Your Reach*, it probably was not a far reach in intuition for me to wonder what else he might have written.

In addition, one trait that Bill Bottum and I clearly shared was a certain packrat mentality. Both of our homes are filled with a combination of books that we love, along with lots of paper!

All of this offers ample explanation of my two dreams. Still, I know that it was these dreams, rather than my knowledge, that prompted me to contact both George, and Bill's family, and to arrange an initial visit for going through Bill's personal papers and files. I do not think that any of us expected to find much of any writings beyond the couple of documents that we already knew existed—indeed, I recall saying that I was doing this because I needed the peace of mind of knowing that such writings did *not* exist. However, I also know that I was simultaneously elated and unsurprised when, over the course of hours spent going through dusty boxes and old file cabinets in his basement, we began to unearth a growing batch of Bill's writings, written over a period of some forty years.

Some of these documents turned out to be the written

presentation of talks that he had given. Others were pieces written for his own understanding of various topics, much like Robert Greenleaf had done. Some were typed, others were handwritten. In the end, we wound up with over eight hundred manuscript pages of writings; this eventually led to the editing of some, which have now been posted on www.billbottum.wordpress.com.

Robert Greenleaf wrote that for something great to happen, one must be able to dream great dreams. In his own humble yet powerful way, Bill Bottum lived his life in such a way that he not only put his own dreams into action, but he inspired many others to do so, too, through countless encounters with others.

FOR REFLECTION

Have you ever had a dream that you thought to be most fortunate? What was it, and why did it matter to you?

13

TOYOTA SENSEI

Storyteller: *Robert W. "Doc" Hall*

The most dangerous kind of waste is the waste we
do not recognize.

—Shigeo Shingo

I first met Jim in the fall of 1976. He was a young professor
at Waseda University in Tokyo, and then very active in an
industrial group that the university had founded in the 1950s.
Among their activities had been industrial tours to the
United States and other advanced economies that might
help Japanese industry "catch up." He was on a scouting trip
looking for information about material requirements planning (MRP).

Jim was attracted to Indiana University because it was
an academic hotbed for teaching MRP, a relatively new
thing then. I had one of the few credit courses with a lot of
MRP content. In the fall of 1977, Jim returned with three
industry friends to take my operations course featuring a
heavy dose of MRP. He picked my class because I taught
mostly students working in industry, and Jim thought his
friends would relate to them and so be able to pick up the
content more by osmosis.

Two of Jim's friends were from Toyota suppliers who

had just been through Toyota's friendly conversion of their operations to the Toyota Production System (TPS). I found that Jim was a friend of Fujio Cho, later to become chairman of Toyota. Cho and Taiichi Ohno, a pioneer in Toyota's "lean thinking," had recruited Jim and others with knowledge of the system to help them analyze their suppliers' Japanese plants during 1974 to 1975. After the oil shock of 1973, Toyota knew they had to fully convert the suppliers to TPS. Jim was no in-house expert, but he had learned enough about TPS to keep suppliers "between the curbs," and suppliers gained even more in-depth knowledge through regular visits by Ohno, Cho, and others on the TPS "varsity team."

But about that time, software salesmen in Japan had begun to entice suppliers with the siren song that MRP would solve their problems without the process revisions demanded by TPS. Jim and friends were on a quest to resolve this issue.

Curious to know what they hoped to learn, during the semester I began asking questions. We went on tours of local manufacturers who had MRP systems. Jim was not impressed, and he began to describe what had happened in Japanese plants with TPS conversions. At first, I thought he was pulling my leg. He invited me to Japan to have a look.

It was tough scraping up the money for a trip to Japan. Jim helped out by paying me a little for giving MRP lectures in Japan. But the first few visits to Japanese plants were real eye-openers. By the time I saw the third supplier, it was obvious that this was no fluke, and unless American manufacturers got this message fast, the Japanese were going to eat our lunch. Indeed, they had already begun to do so.

And thus, almost entirely by accident, began a thirty-two-year career encouraging the development of what we now call lean manufacturing, promoting the formation of the Association for Manufacturing Excellence, and much else.

Jim was my first TPS sensei. We still talk by phone once a month or so. In retirement, his second career is coaching young leaders in high-tech Japanese companies in the basics of process improvement. They really don't know these basics, and it is a weakness that must be shored up. However, Jim and friends, all retired, also realize that the competitive landscape today is very different from 1980. Just being a low-waste, low-cost producer does not guarantee long-term survival anywhere, and it is woefully incomplete in high-cost economies, so we discuss how companies can reinvent themselves over and over.

FOR REFLECTION

How has an encounter with someone led you to see things differently? How has travel opened up new possibilities in your life?

14

MR. RUDOLPH'S WALL

Storyteller: *Paul Davis*

Let the beauty we love be what we do.

—Rumi

"You have to see participation in action in our cafeteria," the excited human resources manager told me. I was visiting a member organization of the Scanlon Leadership Network and anxious to see what the HR manager was talking about. I was surprised when he introduced me to a giant of a man, a Mr. Rudolph, who was covered in dust, breaking rocks with a sledgehammer in the company's cafeteria. Before me was a construction project like none other I had ever seen. I saw the ubiquitous chairs and vending machines that one finds in such places, but there was also a beautiful painted mural, starting waist high and rising to the ceiling, that depicted the Michigan seasons. The section depicting spring was finished. Right below that section, Mr. Rudolph was building a wall. The effect was stunning, like being in the country, looking out over a stone farm wall into a spring meadow.

It was beautiful, but I had no idea what it had to do with participation or employee involvement. The HR manager told me how the company had sought volunteers to improve the cafeteria, which needed to be remodeled. They had gotten no offers from the two hundred employees who worked at the company, so the company decided to create graphic murals of the people and processes that the company used to make its products. To the HR manager's surprise, no one in the company liked the idea when they heard what the company was planning, and they made comments like, "We work too hard to spend our breaks and lunches looking at graphics of ourselves working." Fortunately, Mr. Rudolph came forward with a solution. He said he knew a local artist who could paint the seasons on the walls for a reasonable amount of money. Mr. Rudolph, who owned a stone quarry, said he would build a wall to complement the paintings.

Most surprising was that Mr. Rudolph had been working for three weeks on the project—the first three weeks of his retirement. Mr. Rudolph told me, "When my wife left me, I was ruined. She took all my money. I did not know who to turn to. The HR manager helped me get my life back together. I eventually met the woman of my dreams and remarried. In my life, God comes first, and the HR manager is second. This is how I can give back."

I asked him how many rock walls he had built and he said, "This is the first one, but I own a rock quarry, so I had faith that I could do it." I looked at the HR manager and wondered how many companies would allow an unproven wall-builder to haul tons of rocks and cement onto their property. The HR manager excused himself to run some errands, and I found myself alone in the dusty cafeteria with Mr. Rudolph. He began to explain the meaning of the wall.

Pointing to one of the rocks, he said, "See this rock? It doesn't fit well with the others...Remember that some people are like that."

"See this rock? I tried to shape it and it broke into pieces. Remember that some people are like that."

"See this rock? It is ugly on the outside but beautiful on the inside. Remember that some people are like that."

Finally, he took a rock that he had been working on for a long time and showed it to me. It was the best of the best. It sparkled and shone in the light, as if a vein of diamonds were running through it. He looked at me and said, "It took me a long time to bring the beauty out in this one. Look at it now. It is beautiful."

"Remember that some people are like that, Paul."

FOR REFLECTION

How do you shape others? How do you seek the inner beauty in others? What do you see when you look at another human being?

15

FALLING THROUGH THE HOLE
AT THE BARBECUE

Storyteller: *John P. Schuster*

> If I were to wish for anything, I should not wish for
> wealth and power, but for a passionate sense for
> potential, for the eye, which, ever young and ardent,
> sees the possible. Pleasure disappoints: possibility
> never. And what wine is so foaming, what so fra-
> grant, what so intoxicating, as possibility!
> —Søren Kierkegaard

Going to a barbecue on a hot August day in Overland Park,
Kansas, didn't feel to me like an intoxicating event charged
with possibility. It felt normal, ordinary, and pleasant. I was
going to meet some new people in a familiar suburban backyard, and have casual conversations with people I already
knew, over a greasy, tasty, Kansas City–style meal, with
healthy options for the food-conscious thrown in. I knew I
was going to be with people I cared about professionally, and
was getting to know better personally. I had no idea that this
occasion would end up being the equivalent of passing
through C. S. Lewis's magical wardrobe, which opened up
onto a whole new world of possibilities and potential.

The fifteen guests at the barbeque milled around in the beautiful, shadowed early evening, enjoying wandering conversations in little groups that shifted and re-formed in no particular pattern. I was a consultant in my late thirties who had run my own training, speaking, and consulting practice for seven years. My clients were business leaders, and my specialty was communication and leadership models. I was articulate enough to effectively address many kinds of groups, present important ideas about leadership and management to them, and offer them insights on how organizations run. I was also in the very early stages of executive coaching. Before we called it coaching, we called our sessions "one-on-ones," and I coached CEOs of about twenty companies in Kansas City and Cincinnati as part of my business.

I loved my work, even though it required intense effort and a lot of time. One reward for me was learning. As an English major, former teacher, and social worker—who had also had seven years and a human resources leadership role at the U.S. Department of Environmental Protection—I had never worked in the private sector until I started my own business. This work effort had become a major way I was encountering the planet—traveling the world, encountering its cultures, meeting people, and experiencing Earth's ever-expanding story.

I was a "northeast" thinker, like most business people, meaning the trend lines on the chart of my life were always heading up and to the right on the x and y axes. And I was in the additive time of life—my thirties, in the first half. I could only think of more and bigger: bigger audiences, bigger fees, more clients, more important work, and all the growth that thirty-somethings project for themselves. I had accomplished two things in my vocational/career efforts to this point:

I had found out some of the things I was good at and could be paid for. That in itself was not easy, as my twenties had been filled with career wanderings and identity puzzlement.

I was deep in the life stage of making my mark in the world and trying to establish myself in the high-influence echelons of my profession, which I hoped I deserved.

THE FORTUITOUS INVITATION

Back to the barbecue.

I ended up having a conversation with a consultant named Kathleen Smith. I did not know her well, but she was my age and had a reputation for being gifted. She was the main host of the gathering. She was the one who opened up the wardrobe door. Kathleen said it this way: "John, there's this guy out in Santa Barbara who has a good organization. It's called the Mid-Career Development Institute. His name is Frederic Hudson, and he puts on important workshops. I really recommend that you go to it."

Always on the quest for new material and models to make my speeches and training better, I was interested in spite of not having a lot of detail. I don't read *Consumer Reports*—intense analysis before I buy is not my pattern. After gathering some data, I tend to go with what feels right. Perhaps I trusted Kathy in spite of not knowing her that well. Besides, I was in seminar-material-acquisition mode all the time. Without enough discrimination on my part, I would check out anything in the marketplace of ideas that could make my presentations deeper, funnier, more insightful, more accessible. I was a restless seeker. I had found some rich veins and real gems in unexpected places during my eight years of business.

A few months later and a bit intoxicated by possibility, Patricia—my wife and partner of two years—and I found ourselves on a plane headed for Santa Barbara for a workshop at the Mid-Career Development Institute.

The barbecue conversation with Kathleen Smith was one of my life's important fortuitous encounters, because it led to the workshop that changed my view of my work, my life, and me. In his book *Letters to a Young Poet*, Rainer Maria Rilke wrote haunting and now-famous lines about how we grow: "The future enters into us, in order to transform itself in us, long before it happens." My future had presented itself to me over some barbecued chicken and through a conversation with Kathleen, whom I then did not see again for almost twenty years. But her invitation lived with me daily since I took her up on it.

THE BEGINNING OF THE END OF THE FIRST HALF OF MY LIFE

How did the conversation and the following workshop with Frederic Hudson change me?

A flash-forward twenty-plus years can help answer that. I grew from the consultant/trainer version of me at the barbecue to what I do now: coach and mentor executives, speak and stay active on sustainability issues, play guitar and sing, and write. And I do one other thing: I have the honor to teach professional coaching to future executive coaches at both the Hudson Institute of Santa Barbara (the name that was adopted by the Mid-Career Development Institute about a year after I met Frederic Hudson) and at Columbia University's coaching certification program, where the world comes to get coaching skills.

The field of coaching is much more about listening and evoking than it is about presenting great material. It relies on the power of your presence and the quality of your character more than on the great models you can pack and integrate into your head. The "C. S. Lewis wardrobe" that Kathleen showed me in her backyard turned out to be the portal for my journey to becoming a mentor and coach. And my journey is but one idiosyncratic version of the universal journey we all must take in the second half of life, the journey that is less about linear, success-oriented, "northeast" thinking, and more about soul and vocation and cycles.

So how exactly did the workshop change my view of life and work?

Frederic's workshop was founded on carefully crafted and well-researched models of adult human development. I had not studied that field before and, like 99.9 percent of the population, had made no real application of important knowledge about how adults grow to my life or work.

My "northeast" thinking was just one example of that. The workshop ended many of my old ways of being and working, but also opened up possibilities for new ways. The workshop was—

— the beginning of the end of my believing that podium power and being a "sage on the stage" was my primary career target, and instead the realization that I could also be a "guide from the side";
— the beginning of the end of my thinking that great material would make my career sing and that powerful on-target articulation was my greatest gift;
— the beginning of the end of the idea that life had to go northeast for me to feel happy, and instead the lesson that life goes in cycles;

— the beginning of the end of my conclusion that doing and results were foremost, and instead the realization that effective *doing* is based on the quality of one's *being*;

— the beginning of the end of my trying to be delightful instead of transformational;

— the beginning of the end of an identity for me as a person who lived on the *outside* of himself versus a person who wanted to live *from the inside out*;

— the beginning of the end of the energies that had informed the first half of my life; and

— the beginning of the end of my wading in the shallower waters of motivation theory in business, and instead the beginning of my launch into the deep human yearning for fulfillment through answering the call to leadership, transcendence, and self-expression.

Needless to say, the workshop had an impact. In fact, several months later, Patricia and I went again. (Patricia and I even took her mom, Audrey, aged seventy-two and facing retirement, to the workshop. Audrey needed to form a plan for her post-retirement life.)

I started studying deeply with Frederic, who was also a founder of the Fielding Institute, which was based on the process of human growth and transformation, and which he knew inside and out. One of the main messages he said to me was, "The quality of a person's life is dependent upon the quality of their inner dialogue." So I became a student of the inner dialogue. Frederic was teaching me that the inner dialogue, that intimate conversation with one's self that a coach gets to join and enrich, is the determining factor for leadership and for life, the factor that mattered. Frederic also told me, "John, you need to be more psychological." I wasn't totally sure what he meant at the time, but knew it was a challenge to my depth. My previous professional superficiality had pushed me toward the podium and a kind of "rah-rah, speaker-trainer" attitude, causing me to ignore my own depth as a human being. I still enjoy my frequent trips to the podium because I do have a bit of the showman/artist in me. But I'm now at the podium to do my best at sharing my depth, along with my latest material, my experiences, and my reading.

I attempt to be more "psychological" in the sense that Frederic prescribed. Podium and presence, coaching and listening, are the states of being upon which I base my material. My writing has also become deeper. My book *Answering Your Call* is about the everyday psychology of living from your essence in the common roles that you assume: parent, manager, professional, neighbor, and so on.

In a word, I welcome any success that my doing makes available; I work at being present to my own and other's lives.

So that was my fortuitous encounter. Kathleen's barbecue in Overland Park was the wardrobe. It was the hole through which Alice fell and that deposited her in another world. And to pile on the allusions (with apologies to C. S. Lewis, Lewis Carroll, and now George Lucas), Frederic became my Yoda, since I, like Luke Skywalker and many adults still searching out their path, had been almost as clueless about my true identity.

The barbecue transported me to the other side of my life and of my thinking, to a total transformation of my perspectives.

Fortuitous encounters. The universe has holes in it everywhere.

FOR REFLECTION

What memory from your past, one vaguely or vividly remem-bered, deserves another review by you to distill its essence and to teach you anew? One gift of memories is that we can go back to them again and again, and with our spiritual imagination, find deeper and fresh applications. Do that now...Find a deeper mean-ing in a memory of a conversation, an encounter, an event, that popped you out on the other side of your life. Once you do that, go share your story with a friend or your partner, and listen to one of theirs.

16

FORTUITOUS ENCOUNTERS OF THE WORST KIND

Storyteller: *Tom Haag*

Everyone has a plan 'till they get punched in the mouth.

—Mike Tyson

How can a fortuitous encounter be "of the worst kind"? It sounds of an oxymoron. Of course, there are many excellent fortuitous encounters of the best kind. I could tell a story of great business success that came from an encounter under communism in Russia (of all things). But a fortuitous encounter related to business success often carries an air of financial greed over personal triumph.

I could tell how I met my wife and the series of incredible incidents that took place in order for it to happen. But these stories are a bit mundane to those who are unable to relate to them. Besides, they're found in every movie with a love story.

No, I have chosen a fortuitous encounter with a man I still do not know to this day. Nor will I ever see him again. He lives in my mind, where I get an occasional reminder of my encounter. Well, you see, I really don't even know who he is!

How is it possible that someone I do not know can have such an influence?

It started in my younger years, and I am now forty-seven, so it was quite a while ago, and it still rings true as a turning point for me in my life. I was a college student in my second year at Kent State University—still young enough to think I was invincible and naive enough to think I could carry on without being too serious about life and where I wanted to go.

In those days, it was legal (and now I know why it is not) for college students to spend the evenings carousing, making the rounds of the pubs and bars downtown, and having more than a few beers. This, of course, meant it was only a matter of time before some mischief occurred; the odds were 1 to 1. Naturally, I was intent on keeping those odds steady.

It was under just such circumstances that I was suddenly the recipient of a punch that I had no time to prepare for. A sucker punch, as it's called.

One sucker punch? What could it do to change a person so much? Well, it was not just the punch; it may have been the bloodied nose, the black eye, or the chipped tooth that resulted from that punch.

A bloody nose is done in one hour and you clean up. It's not so easy to clean up a black eye. Especially when you are expected to visit home that weekend to see your parents and you have to explain what happened. When your friends greet you, it is like a badge of courage. In reality, I realized I was just an idiot. What did I do about explaining it to my parents? Well, I did what any red-blooded, courageous man would do...I didn't go home for two weeks until it cleared up. A simple plan to solve everything!

The tooth? Well, that doesn't "heal." An expensive trip to the dentist may have cured the problem after an hour in a chair, but not for long. You see, when a front tooth breaks off, there is not much for the dentist left to fix. He or she can bond a filling to the flat surface that remains, but that is not the everlasting tooth. As a matter of fact, I have probably had to return to the dentist four times at five-year intervals because the filling just keeps falling off!

Every time this happens, I rue the day I got out of the car, but it also reminds me of how important it is to remain on my path. Have fun, but remain on my path.

But those are the physical effects of my encounter with a fist. Yes, that's right; my fortuitous encounter was with a body part...a fist in the face. I was out with my college roommates. A verbal discussion with the occupants of another car over "rights" to an empty parking place had escalated into heated words, and everyone was trying to prove that his level of testosterone was greater than the next guy's. Finally someone said, "Let's get out of the car!"

It sounded like a great idea. I reached for the car door to open it and make my stand. The stand never occurred. I don't think my head made it past the door frame when my unnamed assailant hammered his fist in my face.

Mike Tyson once said, *"Everyone has a plan 'till they get punched in the mouth."*

My plan changed at that very moment, my fortuitous encounter. It happened so fast I sat back down and was holding my bloody nose before my roommates had even gotten out of the car. Then it turned out that one of my friends knew one of their friends, and everybody decided to call off the scuffle. That left me in the backseat with a senseless bloody nose, an anticipated black eye, and a broken front tooth. (Echoes of *Dumb and Dumber* ring through my head.)

Everything became clearer to me after that incident. I realized that I was just a human being, not Superman. I realized that I was in school for a reason, and this was not it. I realized that senseless violence has somebody on both ends, and I did not like either end.

Over time, I realized this encounter with an "unknown" person was a turning point for me, and I would use it to my advantage rather than fume, looking for retribution. The basic principle of accountability was driven into my thought process from then forward. I had created the circumstances for this incident to happen. I could create the circumstances to build upon the event and make sure that it would not happen again.

Today, where accountability seems to elude virtually every aspect of society, are you making yourself accountable for your own life? Accountable for your decisions? Who is responsible for where you are today? An old sage once said, "Be careful to whom you point your finger when placing blame, for three fingers are always pointing back at you."

FOR REFLECTION

How do you make yourself accountable for your own life? How have negative encounters later become positive in your life?

17

FORTUITOUS ACCIDENT

Storyteller: *Sue Mutty*

One friend, one person who is truly understanding, who takes the trouble to listen to us as we consider a problem, can change our whole outlook on the world.

—Dr. E. H. Mayo

The nightmarish image of the teenage girl flying across the hood of my 1966 Plymouth Valiant is nearly as vivid in my mind today as it was the instant it happened. First the crunch of her bicycle hitting my right front fender; then her head, ponytail, and body in an arc trajectory from right to left; and finally a thud and view of her body resting on the pavement just beyond my left front mirror. As I opened my door and ran to her, I felt certain that I had killed her. I did not. But the deadly image remains with me.

Someone from the gathering group of bystanders called the police and an ambulance from a telephone in a nearby home. Soon the girl began to move and was trying to sit up.

"I'm fine, really. Just a scrub on my knee...I landed on my knee. Where's my bike? Is it wrecked?"

I was still numb from the experience and felt that the people who had surrounded her could help more than I could, so I remained in the background, amazed that she was still alive, much less wanting to stand up and check out her bike.

As I attempted to figure out how this accident could have happened, I felt immense remorse realizing how serious this might have been. I remembered stopping at the red light, looking to my right for pedestrians on the sidewalk, and to my left for the second time for oncoming cars in the lane I planned to turn into. As I accelerated into the street to turn right, this horrific scene played out in front of me. I never saw her coming toward my car as she rode on the sidewalk against the flow of traffic in the main thoroughfare.

The ambulance arrived about the same time as the girl's mother who lived only a few blocks away. The girl insisted she was fine, could stand up with a little help, and just wanted to get back on her bike. Ambulance attendants cautioned her mother otherwise, preventing further injury to what turned out to be a broken knee. After the police took information from the teenager, she was released to her mother for a visit to the emergency room.

My memory of my interview with the police is blurred. I know I was still in shock. That "cold all over" feeling that comes with a rush of adrenalin remained with me. I could barely accept the fact that I did not receive a ticket...I had hit a bicyclist with my car! The police explained that they had seen a number of these bike accidents since the implementation of the "right turn on red" law in Michigan, especially in a college town where students were somewhat negligent of the rules of the road for bicycles. The girl did have the green light, but she should have been riding in the street with the flow of traffic, not on the sidewalk against the flow. Somehow, that didn't absolve my guilt.

The event was over, and not as horrible as it had originally appeared. Even though the accident itself is still clear in my mind, what has stayed with me in an even more influential way is what occurred as I was leaving the scene. As the police and ambulance drove away and the bystanders dispersed, I was approached by the one witness who had also spoken with the police.

When I got to my car, he opened the door for me and said, "That must have been horrible for you to see that young woman on the pavement like that. How frightened you must have been!" He continued, "You must have been so relieved to know that she was not critically injured. Are you concerned about driving to your destination from here? You might be feeling guilty, but remember you and that young woman share responsibility for the accident. She is going to be okay. Are you?"

The dialogue continued for just a few minutes. He questioned, listened, reflected. I talked, got in touch with my feelings, and calmed my emotions.

I had never felt so cared for and understood by a complete stranger! His insight and intentional listening to my feelings and my responses in that moment were powerfully comforting. In only a few minutes of conversation, I was more composed and ready to proceed with my day.

As an undergraduate resident assistant at Michigan State University, I had been trained in empathy and reflective listening, and I understood it to be an effective tool for helping college students in all sorts of problem situations. As this bystander interacted and used these same communication skills with me, I transitioned from a state of shock to a more calm and rational person who could get back in the car and drive. The rubber knees and shaking hands became steady, and my feelings of guilt subsided. I will always remember and be grateful for the gift of this stranger's time and empathic attention, and always treasure its powerful impact.

Had I not had this accident and this experience with a person I never saw again in my life, I might have never given proper attention to the usefulness of empathy and reflective listening in many areas of my life. In the thirty-plus years since that day, I have used these skills in my roles of parent, trainer, facilitator, consultant, manager, and friend. As a professional facilitator, I have used empathic listening to help me lead groups with disparate perspectives to join in common goals and shared meaning. It has been a critical component of much of the highly respected parent-effectiveness training, leadership training, and interpersonal-relationship development that I have delivered to thousands of workshop participants. Empathic listening creates a feeling of acceptance and understanding when individuals feel alone and misunderstood. In interpersonal conflict, empathy can build understanding of behaviors when individuals can label the feeling that drove conflicting words and actions.

Most highly regarded leaders are men and women who demonstrate competence in this interactive domain. When we think of people who really connect with others as leaders, managers, colleagues, and friends, it is likely that this skill is second nature to them and is frequently a component of their everyday interactions. In the absence of empathy, leaders are often viewed as distant and uncaring. It can be the crucial difference in breaking or building successful careers and effective relationships

I was fortunate to become a more dedicated student of this remarkable skill as the result of a very frightening and unfortunate circumstance. For the long term, its impact and the influence of the stranger who helped me learn it has been even greater than the memory of the event itself.

FOR REFLECTION

How does listening create positive encounters with others in your life? How can demonstrating a skill become a fortuitous event for others?

18

LEGACY

Storyteller: *Larry C. Spears*

There are certain things that are fundamental to human fulfillment. The essence of these needs is captured in the phrase: to live, to love, to learn, to leave a legacy. The need to live is our physical need for such things as food, clothing, shelter, economical well-being, health. The need to love is our social need to relate to other people, to belong, to love and be loved. The need to learn is the mental need to learn and grow. And the need to leave a legacy is our spiritual need to have a sense of meaning, purpose, personal congruence, and contribution.

—Stephen Covey

I have been fortunate to have had two mentors in my life. One was Bill Bottum (see chapter 12), whom I knew from 1990 until his death in 2005. The other was Stevens (Steve) Brooks. The fortuitous nature of that connection began for me in 1976 at the age of twenty. It ended thirty-four years later with Steve's death in June 2010.

These were some of the facts of Steve's life noted in the obituary that appeared in *The Philadelphia Inquirer*:

Stevens E. Brooks, 68, of Chestnut Hill, executive director of the Philadelphia Center from 1973 to 2007, died of complications from pulmonary embolisms at Penn Presbyterian Medical Center on Thursday, June 3, 2010.

Mr. Brooks began working for the Philadelphia Center in 1968. Founded a year earlier by the Great Lakes Colleges Association, the Center offers college students a semester of "experiential education." Mr. Brooks was its director of education until 1973, when he became executive director.

At his 2007 retirement, he commented that in the 1960s the Center had attracted students who wanted to be "agents of change" and to "affect society in positive ways." "What was radical then is now mainstream," he said.

During the 1970s, Mr. Brooks taught filmmaking in Saturday classes at the Philadelphia Museum of Art. He also was on the adjunct faculty for classes in Germantown, affiliated with the Antioch-Putney Graduate School of Education.

Mr. Brooks was a founding member of the Council for Adult and Experiential Learning, the forerunner of the National Society for Experiential Education, which named him one of its three pioneers of the year in 2005.

Mr. Brooks edited the 1979 book *Enriching the Liberal Arts through Experiential Education*.

Many stories of fortuitous encounters can be readily understood through the lens of personal legacy. I'd like to share with you several instances of Steve's legacy that gets to the heart of who he was.

TEACHER

In 1976, Steve introduced me to art films, short films, and documentaries through a one-on-one independent seminar. I was twenty years old, a DePauw University student who had come to the Philadelphia Center—which back then still bore its original name of the Philadelphia Urban Semester —for an adventure in experiential learning. I had heard the day I arrived that Steve was quite knowledgeable about film. I loved film and writing, and I had begun to write film reviews, and thought it would be an interesting experience to do a lot more of that. I sat down that first day and wrote a short proposal in which I asked Steve if he would allow me to do an independent study with him. Steve happily said yes, and I was thrilled.

Over the course of the next twelve weeks or so, I checked out several films each week from the Philadelphia Free Library and viewed them on an old film projector at the Philadelphia Urban Semester office at 1227 Walnut Street. I wrote reviews of each of the several dozen art films and documentaries that I saw. Luis Buñuel's *Un chien andalou* (1929), François Truffaut's *Jules et Jim* (1962), Charles Braverman's *Condensed Cream of Beatles* (1973), and many other films that I watched linger in my mind as wonderful memories from that one-on-one study. Steve and I sat down once a week and discussed both the films and my written reviews. That independent study turned out to be a great experience in a number of ways—and it was the beginning of a relationship with Steve that lasted thirty-four years.

MENTOR

In 1979, I proposed to Steve that the Philadelphia Urban Semester create an alumni network, and he agreed. Over the next eight years, I worked ten hours a week, in addition to my full-time work elsewhere, creating the Philadelphia Urban Semester Friends, tracking down mailing addresses, producing newsletters, and organizing several reunion events. I loved the work, my contact with alumni of the program, and my frequent interactions with Steve during those years.

Beginning in 1980, I consciously began to view Steve as a great mentor and sought to learn all that I could from him. Steve had what industrial psychologists would consider well-developed executive capacities. He was even tempered—I rarely saw him show anger. He enjoyed his work and the people with whom he worked. He was generous with his time and with his ideas. He held onto the reigns of leadership loosely, not tightly, a great trait that allowed considerable creative freedom for those who worked for him.

Steve was especially comfortable with students in the program, and he interacted with more than seven thousand of them over a nearly forty-year period. It was always my feeling that being around students helped to keep Steve young.

In 1987, I was appointed executive director of the Greater Philadelphia Philosophy Consortium, a program based at Bryn Mawr College, and thus ended my work with the Philadelphia Urban Semester, but I learned much from Steve's mentorship during those years and after.

FRIEND

In 1990, my wife, Beth, and I moved to Indiana when I was appointed president and CEO of the Greenleaf Center.

When our second son was born later that year (joining his older brother, James), we named him Matthew Stephen Peter Lafferty Spears. We chose the name of Stephen with two Steves in mind: Steve Brooks, and my guitar hero, Stephen Stills.

I had business trips to Philadelphia a couple of times a year and would visit with Steve at the office whenever I was in town, oftentimes having lunch together at Portofino Restaurant, downstairs from where the old offices had been. In time, my visits resulted in a new relationship with Steve—we became friends.

At some point, I began to stay with Steve and Krail, his wife, whenever I came into to town. Both Krail and Steve were always the most gracious of hosts. The three of us had many wonderful dinner conversations together. After dinner, Steve and I would often stay up late and talk about the old days, about our current work, and especially about our hopes and dreams of things to come.

SERVANT-LEADER

In 2008, I launched the Spears Center for Servant-Leadership and asked Steve if he would join our Council of Equals (our board). I was most grateful when he said yes. At the council meeting held just a few weeks before his death, Steve was experiencing several health problems; however, he and Krail came out to southern Michigan where we spent several days together at Sunnyside, a lovely retreat center in the Irish Hills region, and at Cherry Point, where Paul Davis's family has a cheerful lakeside home. I was temporarily on crutches at the time with an injured foot, and Steve was using two canes as an aid in walking. We commiserated and laughed over our predicaments. I miss his wise counsel and superb storytelling.

LEGACY

Steve Brooks left a considerable legacy through his service and leadership:

> The Philadelphia Urban Semester remains his greatest professional legacy, having influenced seven thousand college students and many others.

> His leadership in the field of experiential education is a great intellectual legacy.

> His numerous friendships, and especially our own thirty-four-year friendship, are a personal legacy for which I am eternally grateful, and which I feel most fortunate to have had.

> And, of course, one of Steve's greatest legacies is the love he had for his wife, son, and other family members.

The Stephen Covey quote at the beginning of this chapter describes Steve Brooks quite accurately. He was committed to living, to loving, to learning. Through it all, he left a legacy that lives on in the world, and in the hearts of many who knew him.

FOR REFLECTION

What legacy do you hope to leave to others? Do you imagine ways in which you can serve and lead others as a mentor and a friend?

ABOUT THE AUTHORS

LANE BALDWIN

As a musician and songwriter, Lane Baldwin has toured the world and recorded with dozens of artists. His servant-led band Deeper Blues preaches a message of community to share the pain and the healing power of Blues. As a business consultant, he promotes servant-leadership and humanistic management practices to others while using them to guide his own companies. As a writer, poet, and speaker, Lane offers a message of living in harmony and finding fulfillment in the service of others. As a person, he's just trying to be the best human being he can be. Learn more at www.lanebaldwin.com, www.lanconbass.com, www.servant leadershipsolutions.com, and www.lifewithspirit.org.

PAUL DAVIS

See "About the Editors."

BECKY FULGONI

Becky is VP for People and Manufacturing at Landscape Forms, Inc., a world leader in public space furniture (www.landscapeforms.com). Recognized by the *Wall Street Journal* as a "Winning Workplace," Landscape Forms is a leader in lean high-involvement workplaces. Becky serves on the board of the Scanlon Leadership Network. Becky is also an accomplished artist, designing clothing that she sews herself.

TOM HAAG

Tom is president and CEO of SGS Tool Company (www. sgstool.com). SGS has won awards as a top-supplier, high-involvement entrepreneurial organization and is featured in the book *Results Rule* by Randy Pennington. Tom serves as chairman of the Scanlon Leadership Network Board of Directors. When not working, Tom can be found raising his family and enjoying major and minor league baseball.

ROBERT W. "DOC" HALL

Doc is professor emeritus of operations management, Indiana University. He was a founding member of the Association for Manufacturing Excellence and editor emeritus of the association's publication, *Target*. Dr. Hall was one of the first examiners for the Malcolm Baldrige National Quality Award. Currently, he is an examiner for the Pace Award (for innovation among auto industry suppliers), the AME Best Company Award, and Industry Week's Ten Best Plants awards. His newest book is *Compression*, on the need to completely revise business thinking to take performance to the level necessary for the twenty-first century. To learn more about Doc's work please visit www.compression.org.

RICHARD J. LEIDER

Richard J. Leider is founder/chairman of the Inventure Group (www.inventuregroup.com), a coaching and consulting firm in Minneapolis, Minnesota, devoted to bringing out the natural potential in people. He is also author and coauthor of eight books including the best sellers *Repacking Your Bags* and *The Power of Purpose*. In addition, Richard Leider and Larry Spears are coauthors of several essays including "Savoring Life through Servant-Leadership," "The Heart of Giving," and "Seekers Anonymous."

MYRON MARSH

Myron Marsh is the retired CEO of Thomson-Shore, an employee-owned printing company (www.thomson shore.com). He currently serves as chairman of the board. Thompson-Shore has won numerous awards in the printing industry for its high-involvement culture and its leadership in "green" printing. During his long career, Myron worked for three different Scanlon companies, and served on the Scanlon Leadership Network Board of Directors. He was given the Scanlon Stewardship Award in 2006. Myron is an avid cyclist and bibliophile.

SUE MUTTY

Sue Mutty is an independent human resources professional in Lansing, Michigan, and an adjunct faculty member at Lansing Community College. For more than twenty-five years, Sue has worked as a performance-improvement consultant. She is a member of the National Association for Female Executives.

JOHN P. SCHUSTER

An "evocateur at large," John is an author, executive coach, mentor, and speaker. He serves as faculty in coaching at

Columbia University and is senior faculty for the Hudson Institute. He is the creator of Profit & Cash®—a board game to teach financial literacy, which has been played by almost half a million people. His book *Answering your Call* is a guide for living your deepest purpose. John's Web site is www.johnschuster.com.

LARRY C. SPEARS

See "About the Editors."

ABOUT THE EDITORS

PAUL DAVIS

Paul Davis served as president of the Scanlon Leadership Network from 1993 to 2008. Since his retirement, he continues to consult, volunteer, and write through his work with EPIC-Organizations (www.epic-organizations.com).

A frequent speaker on leadership, Paul has been an invitational speaker for the European Foundation, the Academy of Management, the Conference Board, the Japanese External Trade Organization, the American Society for Training and Development, the Ecology of Work Conferences, the Greenleaf Center Conference, and DYAD Development of South Africa.

He has worked with Scanlon Network members throughout North America—consulting, training, and developing Scanlon programs and services. He created the Scanlon 101 Program and the Scanlon Leadership Program. He created the E.P.I.C. Culture Inventory™ and the Scanlon Roadmap learning map. He assisted in the development of the Network's Listening Program, the Lean Sim Machine™, and Hoshin Quick Start™. He helped in the development of Scanlon Plans at Watermark Credit Union, ELGA Credit Union, and United Building Centers.

His article "Leadership from Theory to Action" appeared in the quarterly business magazine *Leading Edge*. His article "The ABC's of Gainsharing" appeared in *Physician*

Compensation and *The Employee Ownership Law Review*. His article "Hoshin Planning" appeared in the *Lansing Business Journal*. He coauthored with Dow Scott and Chuck Cockburn "Scanlon Principles and Processes: Building Excellence at Watermark Credit Union," which appeared in the *World of Work Journal* and *Incentive Compensation*. Paul received the Scanlon Stewardship Award in 2007.

Fortuitous Encounters is his third book collaboration with Larry C. Spears. Their other books are *The Human Treatment of Human Beings* (2009) and *Scanlon EPIC Leadership* (2008).

LARRY C. SPEARS

Larry C. Spears is president and CEO of the Larry C. Spears Center for Servant-Leadership, Inc., established in 2008 (www.spearscenter.org). From 1990 to 2007 he served as president and CEO of the Robert K. Greenleaf Center for Servant-Leadership. Spears had previously been managing director of the Greater Philadelphia Philosophy Consortium, a cooperative association of twelve colleges and universities in the Philadelphia area. He also served as a staff member of the Great Lakes Colleges Association's Philadelphia Center and of the Quaker magazine *Friends Journal*, in Philadelphia, Pennsylvania.

Spears is also a writer and editor who has published hundreds of articles, essays, newsletters, books, and other publications on servant-leadership. Dozens of newspapers and journals have interviewed him, including *Fortune*, the *Indianapolis Business Journal*, the *Philadelphia Inquirer*, the *Washington Post*, and *Advancing Philanthropy*. A 2004 television broadcast interview of Spears by Stone Philips on NBC's *Dateline* was seen by ten million viewers.

Larry is the creative force behind fourteen books published since 1995. He serves as the senior advisory editor for *The International Journal of Servant-Leadership* (2005 through the present). He also teaches graduate courses in servant-leadership for Gonzaga University. In 2010, Gonzaga University appointed Larry as its Servant-Leadership Scholar.

Spears is also a frequent speaker on servant-leadership. The titles of some of his addresses include "Servant-Leadership and the Honoring of Excellence," "Servant-Leadership and Business," and "Robert K. Greenleaf's Influence on Trusteeship." Among his recent keynote presentations were addresses to the Servant-Leadership Research Roundtable, the Louisiana Office of Mental Health, Gonzaga University, the Greenleaf Center, and the Friends Association for Higher Education. Since 1990, Larry has given two hundred keynote addresses on servant-leadership on four continents, a dozen countries, and forty states.

Larry has been called today's foremost authority on servant-leadership. He knew Robert Greenleaf and first encountered Greenleaf's writings on servant-leadership in the early 1980s while working at *Friends Journal*. Following Greenleaf's death in 1990, Larry examined Greenleaf's personal papers and discovered dozens of unpublished essays, written over a fifty-year period. Many of these essays were later collected and published in 1996 in two volumes (*On Becoming a Servant-Leader* and *Seeker and Servant*).

Spears has received, among other honors, the DePauw University's 2008 Community Leader Award, and the 2004 Dare-to-Lead Award given by the International Leadership Network. He is also a World Business Academy Fellow. Larry has thirty years of experience in organizational leadership, entrepreneurial development, nonprofit management, and grant writing, having envisioned and authored thirty successful grant projects totaling several million dollars. The Spears

Center for Servant-Leadership is a 501(c)(3) nonprofit charitable organization. It is committed to enhancing the global understanding and practices of servant-leadership.

For more information, please contact:

Larry C. Spears, President and CEO
The Larry C. Spears Center for Servant-Leadership, Inc.
329 Garden Grace Drive
Indianapolis, IN 46239
317.416.8218 (Work)
www.spearscenter.org

*

If you are intrigued by the ideas and stories in this book,
we invite you to share your own fortuitous encounters with us
at www.fortuitousencounters.com.

BOOKS BY
PAUL DAVIS AND/OR LARRY C. SPEARS

Fortuitous Encounters: Wisdom Stories for Learning and Growth. Edited by Paul Davis and Larry C. Spears, 2013.

The Spirit of Servant-Leadership. Edited by Shann Ray Ferch and Larry C. Spears, 2011.

Within Your Reach: The Beatitudes in Business and Everyday Life. Bill Bottum; edited by Dorothy Lenz, George SanFacon, and Larry C. Spears, 2010.

The Human Treatment of Human Beings. John Donnelly; edited by Paul Davis and Larry C. Spears, 2009.

Scanlon EPIC Leadership. Edited by Paul Davis and Larry C. Spears, 2008.

Practicing Servant-Leadership: Succeeding Through Trust, Bravery, and Forgiveness. Edited by Larry C. Spears and Michele Lawrence, 2004.

The Servant-Leader Within: A Transformative Path. Robert K. Greenleaf; edited by Hamilton Beazley, Julie Beggs, and Larry C. Spears, 2003.

Servant Leadership: A Journey into the Nature of Legitimate Power and Greatness. Robert K. Greenleaf; edited by Larry C. Spears, 2002.

Focus on Leadership: Servant-Leadership for the 21st Century. Edited by Larry C. Spears and Michele Lawrence, 2002.

The Power of Servant-Leadership. Robert K. Greenleaf; edited by Larry C. Spears, 1998.

Insights on Leadership: Service, Stewardship, Spirit, and Servant-Leadership. Edited by Larry C. Spears, 1998.

Seeker and Servant: Reflections on Religious Leadership. Robert K. Greenleaf; edited by Anne T. Fraker and Larry C. Spears, 1996.

On Becoming a Servant Leader. Robert K. Greenleaf; edited by Don Frick and Larry C. Spears, 1996.

Reflections on Leadership: How Robert K. Greenleaf's Theory of Servant-Leadership Influenced Today's Top Management Thinkers. Edited by Larry C. Spears, 1995.